T0329370

.

CAMBRIDGE LIBRARY COLLECTION

Books of enduring scholarly value

Cambridge

The city of Cambridge received its royal charter in 1201, having already been home to Britons, Romans and Anglo-Saxons for many centuries. Cambridge University was founded soon afterwards and celebrated its octocentenary in 2009. This series explores the history and influence of Cambridge as a centre of science, learning, and discovery, its contributions to national and global politics and culture, and its inevitable controversies and scandals.

Sketches from Cambridge

Reprinted from the *Pall Mall Gazette* and published anonymously in 1865, Leslie Stephen's *Sketches From Cambridge* provides an affectionately sarcastic glimpse of student life at Cambridge University and its colleges. The wickedly funny prose explores the manners and customs of a variety of student stereotypes of the day. Profiled in these caricatures are athletes, with one chapter filled with typically light-hearted venom devoted specifically to rowers; and mathematicians, philosophers, and those poor wandering souls that pursue the social sciences. The collection is intended to provide a complete natural history of that curious specimen the Cambridge student, and it is brilliantly written by Stephen, a former member of the species. While the Cambridge student's fondness for whist, whiskey and billiards is examined, the distinction between him and the even lower, sub-human student form that belongs at Oxford and other institutions is definitively drawn.

Cambridge University Press has long been a pioneer in the reissuing of out-of-print titles from its own backlist, producing digital reprints of books that are still sought after by scholars and students but could not be reprinted economically using traditional technology. The Cambridge Library Collection extends this activity to a wider range of books which are still of importance to researchers and professionals, either for the source material they contain, or as landmarks in the history of their academic discipline.

Drawing from the world-renowned collections in the Cambridge University Library, and guided by the advice of experts in each subject area, Cambridge University Press is using state-of-the-art scanning machines in its own Printing House to capture the content of each book selected for inclusion. The files are processed to give a consistently clear, crisp image, and the books finished to the high quality standard for which the Press is recognised around the world. The latest print-on-demand technology ensures that the books will remain available indefinitely, and that orders for single or multiple copies can quickly be supplied.

The Cambridge Library Collection will bring back to life books of enduring scholarly value (including out-of-copyright works originally issued by other publishers) across a wide range of disciplines in the humanities and social sciences and in science and technology.

Sketches
from Cambridge

By a Don

Leslie Stephen

CAMBRIDGE UNIVERSITY PRESS

Cambridge, New York, Melbourne, Madrid, Cape Town, Singapore,
São Paolo, Delhi, Dubai, Tokyo, Mexico City

Published in the United States of America by Cambridge University Press, New York

www.cambridge.org
Information on this title: www.cambridge.org/9781108000260

© in this compilation Cambridge University Press 2010

This edition first published 1865
This digitally printed version 2010

ISBN 978-1-108-00026-0 Paperback

SKETCHES FROM CAMBRIDGE.

BY

A DON.

[REPRINTED FROM THE " PALL MALL GAZETTE."]

London and Cambridge:

MACMILLAN AND CO.

1865.

CONTENTS.

SKETCHES FROM CAMBRIDGE.

I.

INTRODUCTORY.

THE world may be divided into the two classes of those who have and those who have not received a University education. With regard to the latter, I can only repeat the remark said to have been originally applied to the small colleges by a member of Trinity College, Cambridge—" They, too, are God's creatures." I think it is a pity that more rays do not emanate from the great focus of intellectual life in England to clear up some of the dark places of the land. Because—perhaps from no fault of theirs—

1

they have not sat at the feast, is that a reason for
grudging them the crumbs that fall from our table?
Undignified as it may appear, I would rather invite
them to come and be edified. I would lift a corner
of the veil which hangs over our venerable courts,
and covers from the profane eye the sacred mysteries
of the learned. I would admit the outside barbarians,
as our Chinese friends call us, at least to the gallery,
though they are excluded from the stage where we
act our parts in life. Something, I know, has been
done. Tom Brown has given us a glimpse of
Oxford as seen from the undergraduate's point of
view. Cuthbert Bede has set forth in *Verdant Green*
certain caricatures which represent, I suppose, the
current popular myths of student life. But neither
these, nor other more ambitious attempts, give the
whole truth; they miss many characteristic features
of one of the most characteristic products of English
society; our Universities have grown with our
growth; they reflect our present peculiarities, and
with them they mingle strangely traditions and
customs brought unimpaired from long past centuries; they are typified by their own habitations;

not spick and span new edifices, fresh from the builder's hand, and neatly adapted to the wants of the passing generation, but ancient and historic buildings, with fragments from the days of the Edwards, additions made under Elizabeth, and restorations and adaptations under Victoria; awkward and inconvenient in some details, but incomparably picturesque, and perhaps still more solid than their mushroom rivals. They cannot be summed up in half-a-dozen plans and elevations, but present continually fresh points of view for the traveller, new nooks and corners for the inquiring antiquary, and an infinite variety of beautiful effects for the painter. Perhaps, then, I am not presumptuous in trying to catch some aspects which have escaped others, and if not to correct, at least to supplement their descriptions.

I am not about to present any credentials of my fitness for the task. I would rather escape notice as a man must do who would reveal masonic secrets; I have no fancy for being torn to pieces by "a hideous rout" of infuriate heads of houses. Were it possible, I would not even say whether I lived on the banks of the Cam, where the greasy stream stagnates under the quaint old bridges and past lovely gardens, like a worthless print set in a golden frame, or where the Isis sweeps in graceful curves past Christchurch meadows, and reflects the most beautiful of all distant views of an English town. Such concealment would be useless. The initiated would at once determine the point. I shall not, however, hint at the special benefactor to whose pious foundation in past years I owe my pleasant retreat. It is enough to say that our college has all that is essential to the ideal of a college. There is the ancient corner of building, half merged in more modern structures, which our founder acquired or did not acquire, together with an adjacent field, from certain monks. There is the less venerable court, which affords a perfect example of Elizabethan architecture. There is the atrocious pile of obtrusive ugliness which some sixty years ago repaired the ravages of a fire. We have of course a hall, which has been restored to show the old oak roof, and a chapel, which causes me to live in daily fear of another restoration and another liberal subscription.

Of course, too, we are "bosomed deep in tufted trees," though, in spite of University commissioners, no beauty lies as yet beneath our towers and battlements. We have a lawn of velvet turf, hitherto devoted to the orthodox game of bowls, but threatened by an invasion of croquet, for female influence is slowly but surely invading our cloisters. Whether, like the ivy that gathers upon our ancient walls, it may ultimately be fatal to their stability, remains yet to be seen.

It has not, however, penetrated to the rooms in which I now snatch a few moments from my meditated edition of a certain ancient classical author. I do not mention the gentleman's name, because, as every resident Fellow with no other definite occupation appropriates one pet author for his labours, the learned would identify me as easily as a racing man would recognize a person described as the owner of Breadalbane or of Gladiateur. In old times, a man was allowed professedly to confine his labours to the consumption of port. It was a sufficient and a creditable occupation. But if you wish at once to do nothing and to be respectable now-a-days, the best pretext is to be at

work on some profound study; it is not necessary that
your performance should ever get beyond a publisher's
list. As a cocked hat, without other costume, gives to
the Haytian nigger an air of full dress, so an intention to write a book on classics or on theology makes
a don fancy himself, and be supposed by others, to
be hard at work. But theology is dangerous, even as
an object in the dim background. It is difficult to
touch it in the most delicate way without receiving
some sectarian tinge. I am, therefore, collecting
materials with a view to beginning, at some future
day, to set about concocting a new edition of a not
very favourite author. This occupation allows me
leisure to contemplate the busy life around me; I
lounge at my window to hear " in college fanes the
storm their high-built organs make." I see the
surpliced congregation gathering to form the picture
which suggested to Tennyson his " six hundred
maidens clad in purest white " (I can't say that that
is precisely what they suggest to me), and I listen
daily to " the thunder of the halls," and the fainter
murmur that proceeds from the lecture-rooms. I
breathe an atmosphere of youthful frolics and youth-

ful studies, of old bachelors prosing, and of all the varied life that swarms in a University town.

My occupation, or my pretence of an occupation, leaves me sufficient leisure to speculate upon the surrounding throng. I have not dropped all relations to the junior members of the University. I can still condescend to give our boat a shout when it makes a bump, and to play an occasional innings at a cricket-match. At the same time, I am painfully conscious that that awful being, the head of our college, is beginning to recognize me as a man and a brother ; he shakes hands with me quite as if I was a fellow-creature. From this middle position, between heaven and earth, I can cast an impartial eye upon all that bear office in this our body, as well as upon those who bear none. I am a University man, and no part of the University is alien from me. Certainly, there is no part for which I do not feel an affection.

By the outside world the University is supposed to consist of a body of students and their teachers. The instruction of undergraduates is considered to be the final cause of our existence. In compliance with this prevailing superstition, I will attempt to sketch our undergraduate life, but I enter a protest against it in passing. Crambe, in *Martinus Scriblerus,* asserted that he could conceive of a lord mayor not only without his horse, gown, and gold chain, but even without stature, colour, hands, head, feet, or any body; upon which his preceptor informed him that he was a lying rascal. Some persons who think of a University as a mere teaching shop may be inclined to make a similar reply to me when I say that its essence would not be affected by the absence both of teachers and pupils. But they would grievously err. Did not Charles Lamb sing the praises of the University in vacation time, when lectures are not, and even St. Mary's is deserted? Did not an excellent friend of mine remark to me the other day,—

" What a blessed place this would be if there were no undergraduates! Mr. Babbage has been driven wild by organ-grinders; I only wish he would change places with me for a day, and see how he likes an undergraduate learning the cornopean below and a boat's supper raging over-head. I would do away with undergraduates altogether."

" And what should we be without them ? "

" We should be a band of brothers, studying science in courts devoted to peace, praying for our founders' souls, and laying down a cellar of sound port wine; none of your noisy boys to make night hideous and to waste good brains in cramming bad ones."

" What would the public say to that ? "

" The public are, as Milton very properly remarked, owls and cuckoos, asses, apes, and dogs."

These views are perhaps not strictly in accordance with the prevalent tone of feeling: our studies will continue to suffer from occasional outbursts of youthful mirth, and our labour be spent upon thrusting knowledge into the youthful mind. Assuming undergraduates to be, if an excrescence, at least a necessary excrescence, let us begin by examining their manners and customs.

Before entering into details, however, I must make the rather obvious remark that a young Englishman at a University is remarkably like a young Englishman anywhere else,—that is to say, he is full of animal spirits, a thoroughly good fellow, and intensely and incredibly ignorant. It was once said of Lord Castlereagh that he had never read a book. The person to whom it was said remarked that, of course, that was a figure of speech; that his lordship must, for example, have read the Bible or *Pilgrim's Progress.* The reply was that the assertion was literally true, that he had never read any book whatever. Whether the saying was or was not true of Lord Castlereagh, it might certainly be applied to many of the youths whose cultivation has been perfected at some of our public schools. Their knowledge of English literature rarely extends beyond those variegated shilling novels which adorn the stalls of railway booksellers. Of the exceptions I shall speak hereafter. Meanwhile, my readers must imagine, for the raw material which our intellectual machinery works up into such a refined product, the first rough healthy English lad whom he meets, and multiply him by some fourteen or fifteen hundred. I will begin by describing one of the most characteristic forms into which they are developed, though one to which undue prominence has perhaps been given—I mean the rowing man.

II.

THE ROWING MAN.

LATE writers upon University affairs have elaborately described one particular phase of University life. Whether it is really the most picturesque phase, or only the most easy to describe, may be doubted. Perhaps the sect of muscular Christians—which derived its chief popularity from the genial eloquence of its reputed founder — has given a temporary prominence to the athletic undergraduate. When Alton Locke visited Cambridge, he regarded it with the stern eye of a chartist tailor. Bloated aristocrats, in the livery of their order, paraded the streets. Words of sacred import, but degraded by their common use as mere names of colleges, were bandied about with improper epithets prefixed to them. On the banks of the

Cam one of these profane scions of nobility rode
the unlucky " snob " into the river, and benevolently
swore at him for getting in the way. But even Alton
Locke, " tailor, chartist, and poet," had a good word
for the boat-races. The youths were rather ignorant,
very brutal, and incredibly given to tuft-hunting.
But, after all, there was good stuff in them. The
clenched teeth, starting muscles, and heaving breasts
of the racing crews showed something more than
mere physical vigour. The blood of the Vikings,
the pluck that won the battle of Waterloo—(would
that the Vikings and the battle of Waterloo could
be buried in one grave together !)—and the various
idols by which the muscular Christian is accustomed
to swear, all rushed into his mind together. He
was thoughtlessly shrieking, " Well rowed, Trinity !"
just as the bloated aristocrat tripped him up. Mr.
Kingsley was, of course, speaking not his own sentiments, but those which were recommended by
dramatic propriety as coming from a chartist tailor.
It is for this reason that he has admitted into his
spirited description various points that do not satisfy
the critical eye : the stroke of the head of the river,

for example, actually smokes a pipe—*horresco referens*
—half an hour before the race. The best of all possible or actual descriptions, however, was given in
Tom Brown at Oxford ; it is the one passage in
the book which is really inimitable, and to it I must
refer my readers if they would understand the thrill
which causes every nerve in an old oarsman's body
to vibrate again when he hears "the pulse of racing-
oars among the willows." For myself, I feel, but
sternly repress, the temptation to attempt the
description of a boat-race. I will only say that
amongst the many varieties of athletic sport at the
Universities—and we have now cricket, fives, rackets,
foot-races, rifle-shooting, gymnastics, and every game
that fills the pages of *Bell's Life*, except the profoundly mysterious "knur and spell"—boating has
a clear pre-eminence, and the boating-man is the
purest type of the genuine University athlete. He
is to the devotees of other amusements what the
game-fowl is to the Dorking, or the carrier-pigeon
to the tumbler. He exhibits all the typical characteristic tastes and habits in their most characteristic
form. Rowing fulfils all the requisite conditions

by which an undergraduate's amusements must be fitted to his liking. It goes on all the year round, and interferes with his studies; it requires a great deal of very hard and disagreeable work; it rubs holes in his skin, raises blisters on his hands, and gives him a chance of an occasional ducking; when pursued to excess, it may even injure his health for life; and it gives him an excuse for periodical outbursts of hilarity, which, if skilfully managed, may lead into scrapes with the authorities. To these charms it adds another which is especially attractive to Englishmen. An Englishman is greedy of enjoyment; he likes to cram into a few minutes what a foreigner would spread over hours; if he means to get drunk, he indulges in strong drinks; he despises the feeble liquids by which the desired goal may be gradually and circuitously approached. A German student, it is credibly reported, has been known to intoxicate himself with Bavarian beer, a liquid which might be expected to produce more risk of bursting than of drunkenness. An English student would as soon think of drowning himself in the great tun of Heidelberg: if he does get drunk, he does it with

a will, probably by a rapid internal combination of
champagne and milk punch. Now rowing has an
analogous charm; the whole interest and suspense
is crowded into some five minutes of desperate
excitement. The two minutes during which the
Derby is decided are sufficiently trying to a man
who has thousands on the race; but the youthful
enthusiasm of the oarsman probably almost balances
the pecuniary interest of the betting-man. Even
the speculator on the turf scarcely knows a keener
agony of suspense when the favourite is challenged
in his last few strides, than the lad who shrieks
himself hoarse on the bank, as the nose of his college
boat buries itself in the foam from their antagonist's
rudder.

> One glorious hour of crowded strife
> Is worth an age without a name,

according to Sir Walter Scott; and the sentiment,
if not quite orthodox, meets with the hearty sympathy of the true boating-man.

Rowing is fortunately not a chronic complaint.
After leaving the University few men keep it up.
A man may play cricket after he has added a cubit

to his girth. He may practice rifle-shooting and
march in the ranks of the " Devil's Own" till he
has developed into a judge or a cabinet minister.
He may hunt as long as he can be lifted on to his
horse. The infection of mountaineering is not even
caught, as a rule, till late in life, and the disease,
like the measles, is more severe in proportion to
the age of the victim. Fathers of families have
been heard to discuss for hours the comparative
merits of the St. Gervais and Grands Mulets routes
to the summit of Mont Blanc, long after advancing
years should have confined their ambition to Prim-
rose Hill. But the rowing man after three or four
years of mental aberration generally recovers his
perfect sanity. He can't " get forward" as he used.
A certain protuberance of figure, strongly suggestive
of Mr. Banting, impedes the freedom of his action.
The modern style seems short and snatchy; it has
not the long majestic sweep of former days. A
crew of enthusiastic dons, known familiarly as the
" Ancient Mariners," sometimes revisit the scene
of their youthful sports. As we swing gracefully
round a corner, I hear some irreverent youngster

inquire with a half-suppressed chuckle, " Who's the fat duffer rowing four ?" and I fancy that my form must have lost some of its earlier grace. When the crew of Ulysses obeyed his invitation to step in, " and sitting well in order, smite the sounding furrows," they probably did not excite the admiration of the youth of Ithaca. Ulysses' own sentiment, that they were not then what in old times they had been, doubtless met with hearty concurrence from the bank. They must have caught a good many crabs before reaching the Happy Isles. We recover from the fever of our youth, but its vehemence is proved by enduring traces left behind. Who can forget the time when the fate of cabinets and armies, the expulsion of Pio Nono or the accession of Napoleon III., seemed to him of infinitely less importance than the decision of the University boat-race ? An exciting election or an important vote in the Senate sometimes fills our streets with a crowd of rarely-seen barristers and country parsons. Amongst them you recognize a pair of broad shoulders and a jovial red face ; your friend is as big as ever round the chest and a good deal bigger round the waist ; his black

coat and white tie, and an indefinable air of clerical
gravity, have not effectually disguised him. He tries
to persuade you that he has come to save the Church,
or to secure the adoption of a petition against the
abolition of church-rates, or of a scheme for theological education. But, after half a sentence of due
wisdom, he inquires,—

" How about the University boat ? "

He scarcely knows whether he says *placet* or *non
placet* to the inquisitive proctor, who demands his
vote ; and half-an-hour later you find him puffing
gallantly along the towing-path in a crowd of undergraduates, and panting out that nobody now can row
such a stroke as Jones of Trinity. He puts aside
your feeble efforts to amuse him by a congenial
discussion on Hebrew roots or the National Society,
and plunges with amazing avidity into half-forgotten
details of boating " shop." He rows his old races
over again, and gives you prescriptions for restoring
Cambridge to its old pre-eminence on the river, till
you suspect him of being the gentleman who writes
as " Argonaut " in the *Field*. The fact is, that the
associations connected with his old haunts have caused

a temporary relapse into his old disease. To-morrow he will be again a domestic parson, teaching a Sunday school. To-day he has got back into his old life. He resided at the University for, say, 800 days, excluding Sundays and vacations. Of those, he passed 790 on the river, and during nine of the remainder he was laid up with a strain caused by his exertions. The remaining day, which he wasted in lionizing his mother and sisters, he will regret as long as he lives. Years afterwards he will date events by the University races of the time. The Crimean war, he will say, broke out in the year of "the eighteen-inch race," *i.e.* the race when Oxford beat Cambridge at Henley by that distance. That race was in fact the most prevailing topic of his meditations during the year. It was the culminating event of a series of which the year was made up. Every morning, at that period, he was up at seven o'clock, and took his tub after half-an-hour's trot. His break-fast, according to a superstition not yet extinct, was raw beefsteak. His supper was oatmeal porridge. He measured his wine (except on occasional jollifi-cations) with the careful eye of a gaoler distributing an allowance. He did not smoke for fear of injuring his wind. The only ornaments in his rooms were cups or "pewters" won on the river. His dress always included the colours of his club. His library consisted chiefly of the *Boating Almanack* and back numbers of *Bell's Life*. He bitterly grudged the hour which he daily devoted to the process of being "crammed" for his degree, and was only partially pacified when he had to solve the small arithmetical puzzles in which examples are taken from the river; for a boating man always loves a small joke. His conversation only varied by referring at one season of the year to the sculls, and at another to the fours; and he always had a party of friends like-minded with himself to discuss such matters over a glass of wine.

After all, this is not an exaggerated account of a certain not uncommon type of undergraduates. Their sphere of thought is somewhat limited; but they are very good fellows, and are excellent raw material for country parsons, or for any other profession where much thinking power is not required.

III.

ATHLETIC SPORTS.

I VENTURE to use in its comprehensive sense the term " Athletic Sports," which for some unexplained reason is generally confined to running and leaping matches ; and under this head I will conclude what I have to say upon the athletic tribe, of whom the rowing man is the typical representative.

I was standing at the Oxford and Cambridge sports, partially sheltered by a corner of the pavilion from the pelting of the pitiless snowstorm, admiring the efforts of the bare-legged, bare-armed, and all but bare-backed University athletes. My feet were imbedded in a freezing mixture of mud and melting snow ; my nose assumed a bright purple hue, and was the most prominent object in my field of vision. Beyond it I dimly caught sight through the snowflakes of wild figures careering at intervals across the field, or heaving weights, jumping bars, and throwing cricket-balls.   Here, I thought, is a fine chance for composing a poetical peroration on muscular Christianity. My ideas naturally took the form of a sermon; the text was the dogma attributed to the devotees of the sect whose strange rites I was contemplating; namely, that a man's whole duty was to fear God, and walk 1,000 miles in 1,000 hours; my discourse was, I believe, divided into the orthodox three heads: first, that such an athlete was, of necessity, a true *man;* secondly, that he was a true University man; and, thirdly, that he was a true Christian.

I have unfortunately quite forgotten the logical process by which I arrived at this last result.   It is indeed only when my mind is specially excited that it becomes sensitive to the delicate logical chain by which the merit of physical excellence is connected with the teachings of the Gospels.   At cooler moments I always fancy that, in accordance with a hackneyed precedent, the preacher must have studied muscularity in the pages of *Bell's Life,* and Christianity in those of Mr. Maurice's sermons, and combined the result. It is difficult to fuse together such heterogeneous elements so completely as to obliterate the line of junction. In one respect indeed the muscular Christians have done good service. The same class who deny to the parson the privilege of hunting because it has a certain flavour of profanity (and of course a parson should not be so wicked as other people), used to condemn all athletic pursuits. With a keen nose for the taint of " worldliness," they detected something wrong in all amusements that rose above the tea-party pitch of boisterousness.

A well-known religious writer in the last century threw away his bat on being ordained, remarking that it should never be said of him, " Well played, parson ! " Parsons have been known in our day to play cricket, and even to run races, without severe reproach. We must give the muscular Christians some thanks for helping on our emancipation. When they went a step further, and discovered cricket to be a Christian grace, I think they

approached the opposite pole of error. I do not
wish, however, to renew a battle that has been
fought often enough, nor to trespass within the
dangerous bounds of theological casuistry. I will
leave muscular Christians in peace for the future,
trusting that they may continue their practice and
improve their principles.

The absorbing interest which our students take
in athletic pursuits has given rise to hostile criticism
as well as to elaborate theories in its defence. Two
friends of mine have shrewdly assailed my occasional
proclivities to such amusement. One of them is a
stalwart giant of six foot three, broad of chest and
large of limb; one of those figures whom the Prus-
sian king would have got by hook or by crook into
his Potsdam guards, and at whom an old captain of a
boat-club instinctively turns a longing eye. He enjoys
the rudest health, and finishes his three solid meals
a day with the regularity of a steam-engine. The
consequence is that, like some other men of Herculean
powers, he interprets every pricking in his thumbs
into symptoms of approaching disease and dissolu-
tion. Years ago, when we were both undergraduates, I

skilfully enticed him to row in the crew of which I was captain. Unfortunately, he became conscious one day that an hour before starting he had consumed a mutton-chop, a pint of porter, and an indefinite quantity of bread and cheese. From that hour he has been beset by an imaginary heart complaint, to which he ascribes all his ailments, and for which he naturally holds me responsible. When he feels an unaccountable headache, the morning after a Christmas feast, he complains pathetically of " that second boat ; " he has never got it out of his constitution, he says, and some day it will be the death of him.

" Why, my good fellow," I replied, " rowing is a fine healthy exercise."

" Healthy exercise ! did it not kill seven of the University crew of 1851 in four years ? "

Now in 1851 there was no University crew ; and, moreover, the story has been told, to my knowledge, of every crew for the last twenty years.

By way of soothing him, I reply,—

" Yes, I know that to be true, for no less than five of the crew have severally assured me that each of them was the only survivor; as for you, however, you are as sound as a bell."

This last unpardonable insult naturally arouses his anger; he overwhelms me with stories of A. B. and C., whose deaths were clearly traceable to their exertions in boat-races. It is in vain that I reply that boating is certainly no antidote to existing consumption, nor to over-indulgence in whisky or mathematics; and that most of the cases mentioned are attributable to these causes.

I fear, indeed, that my position is not impregnable. A man may, and sometimes does, injure himself by excessive muscular effort, and doubtless rowing makes large demands upon the strength. I therefore fail to comfort my friend, who persists in his cheerful view till a couple of pills has restored his confidence. The only consolation that I can administer to anxious mothers is that an easy remedy exists. Adopt a good lowering system with our undergraduates; put them upon a strict prison diet, let them attend theological discourses of a gloomy tendency, substitute water-gruel for wine, and let them never walk on damp grass without changing

their shoes. You may soon reduce their tempera-
ments to a level with those of the flabby students
who saunter about in plaids through the streets of
a German University town, haunting pastry-cooks'
shops and smoking yard-long pipes. You may get
rid of their high animal spirits, and perhaps make
them fitter to teach in a Sunday-school. I will
answer for it that they will not hurt themselves by
rowing or running; whether they will develope any
other undesirable propensities I cannot say. So
long, however, as they are pampered up to their
present pitch of physical vigour, they will continue
to worship physical accomplishments with undue
fervour, and will frequently seek to acquire them by
undue exertions. In fact, the only way to have no
martyrs is to have no saints; if you wish no boilers
to burst, you had better keep the water below boiling
point. For my part, I prefer our present system,
just as I enjoy the pace of an English express train,
though it increases the risk of accident.

The same remarks apply in some degree to the
criticism of the other friend of whom I spoke. He
was in old days my mathematical "coach." He

lived in a set of rooms, surrounded by a lively assortment of such works as Hymer's *Conic Sections* and De Morgan's *Differential Calculus*. His only ornament, a statuette of Newton (apparently in the act of making the remarkable discovery that you can't see through a plaster prism), kept watch over a wild sea of papers, covered with every variety of distorted ellipse and hyperbole and distracted entanglement of symbols. Every alternate day for three terms I had presented myself to be indoctrinated as the clock struck twelve. One day I was half-an-hour late.

"Where have you been ?" he inquired.

"Down the river," I confessed in a moment of weakness.

"You mean that big sewer at the back of the college, I suppose."

I regret to say that this description of the noble Cam is so far true that the prosperity of rowing depends in no small degree upon the tribute derived from the town drains. If their contribution was diverted, an eight-oar would frequently find it hard to turn. I therefore admitted the justice of his remark.

" What ? " he said, meanly adapting to the boat-races the sneer which an ancient dandy first levelled at the House of Commons,—" Does that go on still ? You may count every day spent on the river as a place lost in the Tripos."

I do not mention this to argue against the venerable prejudice which asserts the incompatibility of muscular and intellectual exercise. The prejudice is, indeed, so far true as that few men can obtain eminence in both. We all remember the swell in *Punch,* who accounted for the excellence of his tie by the fact that he gave his whole mind to it ; and now that our various sports have been carried to such perfection, those who pursue them with success have rarely mind enough left for distinguished success elsewhere. I recount the anecdote in order to show what must be a refreshing piece of news to some of my readers : namely, that as in Oxford there were hundreds of voters who had never heard of the author of *Vanity Fair,* so in Cambridge many men pass their lives in complete isolation from rowing, cricket, and all other vanities of the kind. A commissioner of education always discovers a large per-centage of the population who have never heard of the Queen ; an examination of resident dons would probably reveal the awful fact that many of them do not know who is head of the river. Moreover, they are sometimes happy and in full possession of their faculties.

I have only one more fact to mention before leaving my athletic friends. The rarity with which the highest intellectual and physical distinction is combined might be anticipated. But is not the devotion to athletic sports injurious even to the attainment of lower excellence ? Does it not contribute to plucks, and prevent a man from soaring from the third to the second class ? I will only say now that some of the admirers of rowing admit that it does so, but deny that this is an evil. It was argued in a late University pamphlet that the captain of a boat-club received a better intellectual training from his position as captain than he did from studying for the ordinary degree. And, indeed, any one who has tried the experiment will admit that it is a severe trial of the judgment to keep eight oarsmen in due subjection.

IV.

MATHEMATICS.

A TRANSITION from physical to intellectual exercise may appear somewhat violent. If I do not mistake, however, there is a closer analogy than might at first sight be evident between the directions taken by our muscular and cerebral energy. To go no further, we expend a great deal of both upon objects intrinsically useless, and, moreover, their uselessness is often put forward as a recommendation. We don't learn rowing or cricket with a view to turning them to practical account. We are not about to set up as watermen or professional bowlers. A man may occasionally find his youthful accomplishments profitable; as, for example, in starting as a billiard-marker; but

it is not likely that that was his primary aim in
learning billiards.   We are quite content if we have
had our fun, won our little meed of glory, and inci-
dentally developed our muscles.   Now, apologizing
beforehand to philosophers, nothing can be less
generally useful than cricket, except mathematics.
As an amusement it is first-rate.   A man may
spend a happy life in cultivating an almost indecent
familiarity with curves of the higher orders, in in-
vestigating extravagant formulæ, and in exhausting
all the letters of all known alphabets to express his
discoveries.   So he may in playing whist, in solving
chess problems, or unravelling Indian puzzles.   As
a mere intellectual toy, mathematics is far ahead
of any known invention.   Metaphysical studies are
equally absorbing, but they don't even profess to come
to any result, and they are apt to spoil the temper.

Of course, certain branches of mathematical knowledge have a direct bearing upon practical life.
Somebody must be able to calculate eclipses and
investigate the theory of tides, or how could we
boast about modern science ?   And, for anything I
know, there is something besides amusement to be

gained even in the abstruse recesses where the high
priests of mathematics utter mysterious sentences,
in a tongue not understood by the vulgar. But the
true enthusiast rejects and scorns the application of
any test of practical utility. Knowledge, he thinks,
is knowledge; the more remote it is from all contact
with concrete things the better; the special merit
of mathematics is that you can sit in your own room
and spin it like a spider out of your own inside
without ever even looking out of the window. Mathematical theorems have a certain beauty of their own,
which like that of some artistic products, is tarnished
by the introduction of utilitarian ends. However this
may be, mathematical, and indeed all other studies,
are not even professedly pursued for their own sakes.
To have been in love with some women is, we are
told, to have received a liberal education; though
love may not lead to marriage. A three years'
flirtation with mathematics is supposed to produce
the same effect. We may never meet them again,
or meet them only to pass scrupulously by on the
other side. But our minds have been strengthened
and prepared for dealing with other subjects.

When the intelligent foreigner of fiction expresses his surprise at our English devotion to classics and mathematics, this is the answer which is invariably thrown at his head. Your students, he says, are kept hard at work till twenty-one upon matters which nine-tenths of them have utterly forgotten at thirty. They have been filling their minds pertinaciously with a lumber which is only to be consigned to vaults and cellars. Ought they not rather to be supplied with some useful stock-in-trade for future life ? What can be the use of keeping them grinding at this mental treadmill, which is actually recommended by the inutility of its products ? Ah, we reply, see how it strengthens the prisoners' thews and sinews. When we once let them out, there is no nut which they won't be able to crack, and no work which they won't find easy by comparison. We teach classics and mathematics because they are the best of all mental gymnastics. They strengthen the intellectual faculties, as lifting weights and jumping bars strengthen the muscles. If asked why they are the best, we appeal to " all experience "— an appeal to experience being a well-known method of at once refusing to argue, and looking preter-naturally wise.

Of course if we had been in the habit of teaching chemistry, or history, or the art of shoemaking, we should have made the same appeal, and with just the same confidence. Our real motives are rather complicated. This gymnastic theory enters into them, and is not without force; but it is far from being the only motive. It is more of a pretext than of a determining cause. It always reminds me of a stock argument put forward in a different case. People sometimes ask, What is the good of horse-racing? The respectable and ostensible reply is that it improves the breed of horses. Our educational system is supposed to improve the breed of under-graduates, and in very much the same way. An elaborate parallel might be easily drawn between the two systems. The examination is to the under-graduate what the racecourse is to the inferior animal. It is the test of his merits after three years' careful preparation. The senior wrangler is the winner of the Derby. The stables in which the horses are trained are analogous to the pupil-rooms of the

different coaches. Uncertain rumours get about of
the result of private trials. A, who is only a two-
year old, is said to have beaten B, who is the
favourite for the next match. One man has done
too little work in the long vacation, and will have
to go through a severe course of training ; another
has been overworking himself, and will want skilful
management to get him up to the mark. Every
now and then a dark horse is heard of, who is
supposed to have done wonders at some obscure
small college. But the safest test of superiority
is to be found in the public performances at the
larger colleges, where several of the best candidates
meet for preliminary competition. Even there, a
man may choose to run dark, and may astonish
his friends in the final contest of the mathematical
tripos.

The parallel fortunately fails in one respect—that
there is very little money invested in the way of
bets ; the running is, consequently, much truer
than in the more sporting event. Two or three
names can generally be chosen from whom the
winner can be almost certainly selected, and, indeed,

an experienced judge can make a fair guess at the
first ten or twenty. I need not add, that the conditions of the match, days, hours, and subjects of
examination, have been as carefully defined beforehand as the keenest sportsman could desire. The
scrupulous fairness which is essential to the interest
of all competitions, whether on the turf or on paper,
is nowhere more unimpeachable than in. our Cambridge Senate-house.

This analogy suggests that there may be some
resemblance in the motives of the competitors. The
excuse for the turf is, as I have said, that it improves
the breed of horses ; but nothing can be further from
the mind of the individual owner. He would be just
as keen if it were proved to do the breed more harm
than good, although in that case the amusement
might lose its general credit. The predominating
desire is of course to win money, and that is precisely the desire which animates our undergraduates.
They wish indeed to win glory too ; but as the
measure of glory is the amount it will fetch in the
Church or at the Bar, it comes to very much the
same thing. A Fellowship may be reckoned as

worth 2,500*l.* on an average. The prospect of
taking pupils or winning a professorship may be
calculated as worth at least as much more. It may
thus be said that a man who can secure a high place
in either of our two great Triposes wins at least
5,000*l.* in money, besides an amount of glory of
which it is difficult to make an accurate valuation.

This mercantile view of the transaction is not a
very dignified one; but, after all, it is a creditable
one to the University. We can't make a better use
of our endowments than in making them prizes for
learning : and all our late reforms have tended to
render them more available for the purpose. The
removal of the various restrictions upon our foundations has thrown continually larger prizes into the
market. The price of good undergraduates has risen
fearfully, as a tutor lately complained to me. He
used to be able to buy a very fair scholar for fifty
pounds, given in the form of an open exhibition.
The other colleges have taken to out-bidding him.
Fifty pounds will now hardly buy a *senior optime;*
a probable wrangler turns up his nose at anything
under seventy, besides rooms and commons. The

competition of Oxford, where so many foundations have been thrown open, has enhanced prices terribly. The Indian Civil Service appointments have had the same effect. Undergraduates have gone up in the same ratio as cotton since the American war. A poor college does very well if it can snap up a first-class man by some clever manœuvre : as, for example, by securing such a piece of damaged goods as an idle youth, who has promised to work harder in future, or a lad with a defective education, who may possibly develope talent when the experiment of educating him is tried. Some of the consequences of this system are excellent. I know more than one poor man who is maintaining himself at the Universities by the scholarships and exhibitions he has won. And though Adam Smith tells us that in the long run foundations depress the reward of learned men by artificially increasing the supply, the particular cases are pleasant. The effect, however, upon our system of education is a more difficult matter to appreciate, and is less often remarked.

Nobody comes to the University in order to learn. If that is too strong a statement, I may at least say that no one comes with a view to learning chiefly. I remember a rash youth who stated to his friends that he was studying mathematics with a view to improving his mind. It became a standard joke against him ever afterwards. The ordinary under- graduate considered it as equivalent to a confession of idiocy. It savoured of priggishness to proclaim a wish for mental improvement; but to secure that object by means of mathematical study was almost incredible folly.

Indeed, it is perfectly obvious that nothing can be more absurd than to make five hundred young men (about the annual number of freshmen) give up three years to reading classics or mathematics for their own sake. Perhaps fifty of them may be improved by such a discipline. As for the remainder, nothing but custom could persuade parents or sons that the best use to be made of the three years after eighteen is to make ignorant youths into third-rate classics and mathematicians—especially as they are immediately to forget all about it. The " gym- nastic " theory, as applied to those below the first- class, is a mere farce. If our only inducement was the knowledge which we have to communicate, we should have to offer a more varied bill of fare. Fortunately we have a great many others, and we are able to go on quietly with our two old-established dishes, just as a public-house in beautiful scenery can attract visitors, though the only variety in dinner is that they eat up one side of the sheep and down the other. If any one doubts this, he may ask himself whether he would recommend a stupid lad of eighteen living in London, who was to enter a profession in three years' time, to pass the intervening years in attending third-rate lectures on Greek and Latin. If he would, the lad would, I think, be stupid indeed to take his advice.

For those who take to the training kindly, and reach the top of the tree, it is a very different question; for them, I fully believe our intellectual training to be excellent, though even for them it would, but for the endowments, be rather an expensive luxury. It is rather a severe tax upon any man's time and brains to spend three precious years, not in learning something, but in learning to learn something; I repeat, however, that for

those who become really proficient, I believe the
polish attained to be worth the trouble of attain-
ing it.

It will now, I hope, be evident what is the
meaning of our attachment to the old studies. We
have great prizes to give away for learning. Moreover, those prizes are the great stimulus for learning,
and we depend necessarily more upon them than
upon the attractions of the learning itself. We thus
prefer not the studies which are most useful, but
those which afford the best tests of merit. The old
examinations have been carefully and elaborately
worked into a system by long-continued efforts of
our ablest teachers. They now afford a most delicate
and scrupulously fair test of the merits of rival
candidates. It is one, moreover, of which the nature
is perfectly recognized in every school in the country.
Without becoming too technical, I could not explain
all the difficulties ; but it is obvious that there would
be great difficulties in introducing any new-fangled
test in its place. In classics and mathematics, in
short, we believe that we have the best and most
widely-known race-course for rival candidates to run.

It is long, and hard, and perfectly fair, and by long experience we can tell to a nicety who has won and by how much. It is a matter of secondary importance to decide whether it is the best course to develope all the powers of the competitors. But it is very easy to construct a supplementary theory to prove that it is the best, and to slur over the fact that the improvement of learning is not the main object, but the incidental result, of our system. In my next letter, I will speak of its influence upon the manners and customs of the competitors themselves.

V.

READING MEN.

I HAVE endeavoured to point out one or two leading peculiarities of our educational system. To put
it shortly, we do not attempt to educate directly,
but we hold out tempting baits which can only be
won by a process involving education. The best
intellectual wrestler wins the prize, and he must
practise diligently and train steadily to have a chance.
The effect upon the competitors is twofold. Those
who enter for the highest prizes are subjected to a
sharp mental stimulant for three or four years; they
generally learn at least the art of close and patient
thought. With those who seek not to win honour,
but to avoid disgrace, the case is very different.

With them the horse-race, to which I have compared our Triposes, becomes a donkey-race. Their wisest ambition is to be last amongst those not actually disqualified. Their own motive is to avoid the disgrace which traditionally attaches to being plucked. The negro-slave does. as little work as is compatible with not being flogged; when freed, he does as little as is compatible with not being starved.

The " poll " man shuns the condemnation of the examiner as the slave does the whip of his driver, and thinks all arts fair by which the attention of his enemy can be eluded. It is to be feared that when freed from this terror, he finds a very moderate amount of sustenance sufficient to preserve him from intellectual starvation. I must add that in his case, as in the case of the negro, it is impossible to say that he shows any want of sense. The point of view from which we regard education evidently makes it a mere solecism to educate those at all who are not candidates for prizes; it would be like putting a cart-horse in training for the Derby. We encourage their effort, as it has lately been attempted

to encourage the breed of donkeys, by having a public
show, and giving in the examination·list the names
of those who have not disgraced themselves ; but we
treat them to mere scraps and fragments of knowledge, which they will regard with indifference in
proportion to their common sense. It may therefore be anticipated that there will be a considerable
contrast between the different classes of our students.

The mathematician is to the votaries of other
branches of learning what the rowing man is to
other athletes — the reading man *par excellence.*
We all know the ideal representative of the class.
Sir Isaac Newton, sitting on his bedside, with one
leg of his trousers on and one off, meditating on the
solar system, is a typical example.   There is a
certain dismal road, bounded by straight lines,
and crossing a horizontal plane (all roads round
Cambridge, however, answer to this description)
known as the Senior Wranglers' Walk.   It is a
superstition that between the hours of two and four
(the period consecrated to constitutionals,) shabby-
looking youths in ill-brushed, ill-cut garments, are
to be seen crowding the footpath, conversing affably

on abstruse problems, or stopping to draw strange figures on the gravel with the points of their walking sticks. These are embryo senior wranglers. Their habits are supposed to be mainly nocturnal. Their favourite repast is a cup of tea with muffins, and a couple of friends on a Sunday evening. Their conviviality is typified by the very ancient story of the wrangler who, on taking his degree, locked twelve men into a room with one bottle of wine, saying that they should not go till they had finished it. In fact, they inherit the character which our ancestors applied to alchemists—a tribe of semi-insane enthusiasts, venturing occasionally like owls into broad daylight, but ordinarily plunged in the depths of philosophical abstraction. I may say at once that this is, for the most part, a gratuitous libel.

Paradoxical as it may appear, I rather like mathematicians. They have, indeed, one merit which is almost compulsory. Their peculiar subject is so singularly repulsive to the general public that they seldom intrude it into general conversation. A classical scholar sometimes indulges in the hideous practical joke of making a Greek pun at a dinner-table. The surviving custom of the House of Commons sanctions this detestable infliction. Even Colonel Newcome remarked on a celebrated occasion something about " *emollunt mores.*" And those who would resent as it deserved an illustration drawn from the differential calculus, contort their countenances into a fictitious grin, designed to conceal the fact that Greek is to them equivalent to Hebrew. I once knew a man courageous enough once to ask his tormentor for a translation, and it was also the one occasion on which I saw the asker blush.

Now a mathematician conceals his knowledge as a dentist conceals his instruments of torture. Every now and then he glides accidentally into an accustomed form of expression. A friend once told me, in the course of a theological discussion, that his idea of heaven was a sphere of which the radius varied inversely as the holiness ; but I doubt whether he would have repeated the illustration in the University pulpit.

A few little jokes sometimes emerge into daylight from mathematical sources. It is considered facetious to call a certain path the " y d x "—a joke which is beneath interpretation ; and I see that a gentleman has lately been discussing the question of Professor Jowett's salary under an elaborate allegory concerning the evaluation of π.

I am thankful to say that cases of this shameless depravity are rare ; the inverse process is more common ; a small witticism from the outer world sometimes illuminates the barren paths of mathematics. A stern examiner inquires into the results of a " fat fly" crawling up the spoke of a wheel, or of a " very small elephant" rolling a sphere up a perfectly rough plane—the elephant being so small indeed that his weight may be neglected. This class of questions was parodied by a problem concerning two walruses standing at opposite ends of a revolving plane, and winking alternately with their right and left eyes. I fear, however, that I am trespassing somewhat upon the forbidden ground myself. I will only say that the mathematician of real life is a harmless, and even an agreeable being. His supposed incapacity for practical affairs (as represented in the old story of the big hole for the big cat and the little hole for the little cat) does not often exist. A parallel case may sometimes be found. A senior wrangler was leaving my rooms the other day, when I asked him to shut the door.

" Which shall I shut first," he inquired, " the outer door or the inner ? "

But, as a rule, and with the exception of an unaccountable backsliding towards bad puns, they are apt to be strong even on subjects remote from their own.

The mathematical faculty is sometimes developed at the expense of others, and becomes a sort of deformed mental excrescence. A man, who is otherwise dull, may have a morbid capacity for manipulating symbols and figures, just as there are some stupid people who can learn a new language every month, or repeat a University sermon when they have once heard it read. The class of mind which generally comes to the top in our intellectual contests belongs to a man of a very different order. He is of ·the strong, hard-headed, indomitably persevering breed. He is frequently a big North-countryman, able to drink whisky or to wrestle, not spiritually,

but physically, with the same vigour as he applies
to mathematics. He is a kind of intelligent black-
smith, a man whom prize-fighters regret to see thrown
away upon the Church. The model senior wrangler
should have a cross of the gladiator in him ; he ought
to have the physique of Professor Wilson, with his
poetical and sentimental vein extracted, and the
deficiency made up from a shrewd Yorkshire under-
standing. Although, as I need hardly say, few
senior wranglers come up to this ideal, they
generally approximate in some degree to the intellectual part of the picture. They are of a somewhat
rough breed, but one full of vitality and energy ; and
the best of them fill up the gaps between the hours
devoted to their special study by playfully absorbing
two or three supplementary provinces of knowledge.
They have enough spare vigour to get up Shaksperian
criticism, or all the novels that have ever been written,
or the Russian, Arabic, and Sanskrit languages, by
way of sport. Such men, trained like French soldiers
in Algiers for the severest warfare elsewhere, are
perhaps the intellectual product of which we have
most reason to boast. Why it is true, and how far

it is true, that they have not of late years been so conspicuous in other walks of life as was formerly the case, would require further explanation.

The reverse side of the picture is not so attractive. Our unlucky poll men are chiefly remarkable for generating a series of stories which have been repeated *ad nauseam.* The old legends about the youth who told what the whale said to Moses in the bulrushes, and similar anecdotes, are handed down from generation to generation. One's first impression is that they form part of the stock of anecdotes which is an heirloom of the Aryan race. The same stories in slightly different forms may, it is said, be found in the *Arabian Nights,* in the *Eddas,* and I know not where else. They are told in India, in Persia, and in the valleys of the Scotch Highlands. Jack the Giant-killer was an ancient hero, who has been degraded from epic poetry to figure in nursery tales. One is inclined to fancy, in observing the persistence with which these poll stories are repeated and attributed successively to the notorious characters of the day, that they must have belonged to the same inexhaustible fund. They were probably told under the tents of our nomad fore-fathers, and doubtless Japhet had some anecdote setting forth Ham's hopeless confusion between Methuselah and Tubal-Cain. I have myself listened to a legend about examination blunders, told by a Swiss guide (for even Swiss guides have to undergo an examination as to their geographical knowledge) which would imply that the same errors may be re-peated on the banks of the Cam and under the shadows of the Jungfrau.

At the same time it is possible that human stu-pidity may stumble into the same mistakes from time to time, and the same story thus be true in different epochs. I have come across specimens of blunders which are at any rate equal in absurdity to any of the current anecdotes. I can believe in any degree of mental perplexity on the part of the victims to examination. I remember a youth who beat the story about Moses and the whale by an assertion that Jonah's gourd spake to him and reproved him. I believe a story to be authentic which recounts an unpublished addition to the parable of the Good Samaritan. After repeating the Samaritan's saying to the innkeeper, "When I come again I will repay thee," the unlucky examinee added, "This he said, knowing that he should see his face no more."

The commonest examination stories conform to this type. They are simply strange jumblements of indigested fragments left in the memory. There are, however, some which testify to a more refined description of error. A youth whom I once examined informed me that St. John's Gospel was distinguished by a tone of fervent piety, "in which the other Evangelists were totally wanting."

The fact to which these and most such stories testify is simply that most students of this class attach no meaning to their lessons whatever. They consider that they are talking a mysterious language, which has absolutely no relation to common life. They write out descriptions of the common pump (a favourite question), but they never identify the common pump of examinations with the pump in their own back-yards. An examiner once inquired into the use of the inverted cup sometimes introduced into a currant tart. One of his victims, after

describing the theory correctly, added, with somewhat unnecessary precaution, that the cup must not
exceed thirty-two feet in height ; he of course looked
at the tart from a strictly examination point of
view.

Undergraduates, like school-boys, consider their
teachers to be beings animated by a mysterious male-
volence. They may be good-natured by occasional
impulses, but their main object is to enforce a compliance with certain mysterious rites, which are
recommended by nothing but their own arbitrary
will and pleasure. A man does not understand why
he should get up Scripture history any more than
why he should stand upon his head and repeat abra-
cadabra seventy times running. One test is to him
as devoid of reason as the other. Accordingly he
puts off his learning as long as possible, and then
goes to some famous adept in the great art of cramming. The essential peculiarity of this art is to save
intellectual exertion to the learners. The propositions to be learnt are eviscerated of all meaning, and
then, like preserved meats, packed into the smallest
possible formula to be repeated by rote. I vaguely

recollect a Scripture history put into rhyme, of which
the only verses that stick by me are these :—

> Joshua, son of Nun, and Caleb, son of Jephunneh,
>   Were the only two
>   Who ever got through
> To the land of milk and honey.

It is a cardinal principle of judicious cramming
to try the memory rather than the intelligence. I
have known several youths who carried this so far as
to start upon the apparently desperate undertaking
of learning Euclid by heart rather than understand
its propositions. If you endeavour to explain a difficulty, the invariable answer is, "Don't bother me
with explanations ; I will get it up, but I am not
going to understand it." The smallest change of
conditions, such as altering letters in a mathematical
formula, is generally enough to upset this intelligent
class.

I should not be just if I did not add that efforts
are being made to improve this state of things. I
hope they may be successful. Meanwhile, it will
perhaps be evident why I said a few pages back
that some people thought the intellectual training of

the captain of a boat-club better than that which he receives from the poll. It requires much exertion of common sense and judgment, whereas the poll only requires a trifling effort of memory. Moreover, the things thus learnt naturally run off a man's mind, like water off a duck's back, and on looking at them impartially, I am much inclined to think it the best thing they can do.

VI.

THE UNION.

In describing the intellectual and the muscular class
of undergraduate, I have chiefly confined myself to
those who seek glory on the river and in the mathematical tripos.   These are, in fact, the most characteristic products of our soil.   Plants of different
origin are springing up around them with more or
less vitality.   New studies and new sports are being
gradually introduced to diversify the former monotony
of our pursuits; but they have not checked the
vigorous growth of the older forms, nor prevented
them from still affording the purest type of the
genuine Cambridge man.

It is not, however, to be supposed that all our

energy is exhausted in producing mathematicians and
rowing men, nor even in producing all the varieties
of the two classes at the head of which these enthusiasts are respectively presumed to stand. There is
always some vagrant unfixed ability which cannot
show off its paces within the arena chalked out by
official examiners; there are, therefore, a good many
men who consider the recognition which they do
receive to be altogether inadequate to their merits.
We all know the very unpleasant individual who
passes his life without ever getting his talents duly
appreciated. He has a tendency to invent new theories of the universe, to write life dramas, or to make
what the reporters call "lucid expositions" of new
theories of political economy to philosophical societies.
The Ministry have evidently not got their eye upon
him; he makes no way towards the goal of a judge-
ship or a bishopric; and accordingly he revenges
himself upon mankind, not by taking a "pike,"
according to Mr. Weller's innocuous plan, but by
becoming a stupendous bore. That interesting body,
the Social Science Association, provides the intellectual exchange most frequented by the dealers in

this kind of ware; it swarms with unappreciated genius; in every section you come upon bores luxuriating in the novel satisfaction of casting their pearls before kindred bores; damaged and unsaleable mental goods are going off with incredible rapidity.　In fact, the Association acts as a mutual accommodation society, where different members of the great family of bores can talk their own nonsense *ad libitum,* on condition of swallowing the nonsense of their brethren.

　　Now, if you trace backwards the man who effloresces in later life into the full-blown social science orator, you will find that in his earlier days he spoke at the Union.　Examiners, by a curious coincidence, thought as little of his talents as Ministers.　They would no more make him senior wrangler than Lord Palmerston will promote him to the next vacant see; so he generously bestowed his tediousness upon the debating society.　Like the young lion whose teeth and claws are not fully developed, he was not yet armed with that portentous statistical apparatus which now strikes terror into the boldest heart; he had not stuck together that hideous conglomeration of big words which he calls his social theory; but he was able to announce, with his present pomposity, that "all history proves" that two and two make four, and to hurl "scathing sarcasms" against the advancing deluge of democracy. This democratical deluge is, by the way, as great a nuisance as the gulf-stream of scientific bores; it is always lugged by the head and ears (if I may talk of the head and ears of a deluge) into every political argument, in hopes of giving it a philosophical tinge, and generally with a total ignorance of what democracy means.

If all or most of our Unionic orators were of this stamp, I should not attempt any account of their vagaries. The bore who has just chipped the egg-shell is as like the full-fledged bore of later life as a grampus to a whale. There is less of him, but he is as unctuous and tiresome as far as he goes. But the Union debates are often highly amusing, proving satisfactorily the presence of some other element. It is many years since I denounced the Prime Minister of the day as "a contemptible sneak" (or words to that effect), making, as I flattered myself, a smart and rather philosophical remark.

I, of course, cannot now allow my dignity to be ruffled by anything like participation in a debate; but I confess that it gives me pleasure to linger, as it were unintentionally, in a corner of the gallery of what was a Dissenting chapel, and is, for the present, the mimic House of Parliament. From that position of comparative security I can smile benignantly at the quaint coxcombries of rising genius, sometimes laugh at a bit of genuine fun, and retreat precipitately when the bore appears on the horizon.

I need not elaborately describe the characteristics of Unionic eloquence; for I can fortunately point to a living model. An excellent young statesman has lately been treating the electors of Leeds to specimens of eloquence which seemed to come hot and fresh from our walls. He has been laughed at, much as we laugh at a child playing at the occupations of grown-up people, and perhaps we have laughed a trifle too much. All criticism might be summed up in saying that he ought not to have brought his toys into public; but, in their right place, they supplied, as advertisements say, a pleasing entertainment, combining instruction with amusement. The

sailor boys at Greenwich find a ship rigged on dry
land a useful help to learning their art; but they
would not be thereby qualified for immediate service
on salt water. Just so a youth who has been
practising at the Union finds his head swim and
his legs unsteady, and is, in short, altogether at
sea, when he is suddenly brought face to face with
a constituency. He contradicts himself half-a-dozen
times over, for consistency is naturally unimportant
at the Union, where no one is pledged to anything.
He has no objection to violent changes in the Constitution ; of course, a total absence of responsibility
reconciles a man to any changes; and he gets up the
six-pound householders in a morning's walk, just as
a youth would get up, say, the Schleswig-Holstein
question in a couple of hours, so as to satisfy the
critical acumen of a debating society.

All these little proofs of weakness are unnoticed
and unimportant at the Union. I always look on
with amusement, if without awe, at the youthful
eagle essaying his preparatory flights ; perhaps his
wings are not very long, and his flight not very
powerful, but the half-conscious imitation of his

paternal models is always amusing. A youth surrounds himself with a vague halo of semi-official
splendour on the strength of a relation having been,
say, British Minister at a South American republic.
He rises with great solemnity, fills a glass of water,
and places one hand in the breast of his frock coat ;
he proceeds to confide to " honourable members " his
serious doubts as to our relations with the United
States, and even intimates that from information
which he is not at liberty to divulge (this is a dark
hint at the before-mentioned Minister) he has reason
to fear that Mr. Seward has already given orders for
the occupation of Quebec and Montreal.   These remarks are, of course, received with a roar of laughter,
for there is nothing which the British youth detects
so soon and despises so much as an affectation of
premature wisdom.

Indeed, the most characteristic part of our debates
is the temper of the audience.   They exhibit, even
in an exaggerated degree, that sense of humour, or
cynicism, or whatever you please to call it, which is
characteristic of the educated Englishman at all ages.
An Englishman has an ineradicable suspicion of

everything that verges on the sentimental. He
equally despises Yankee addresses to Buncombe and
French twaddle about glory. The model Englishman is the naval captain of poetry, who encourages
his crew by ostentatiously avoiding any appeal to the
higher motives. After a feigned apology for the fact,
in which he obviously glories at heart, that he
" hasn't the gift of the gab," he remarks dogmati-
cally, " That ship there's a Frenchman," and winds
up with the eloquent peroration :—

> If she isn't mine in half an hour,
> I'll flog each mother's son.

This truly national contempt for the " gift of the
gab " becomes modified later in life. We all profess
to hate public speaking after dinner; in consequence
of which we never have a dinner of a semi-official
kind without half-a-dozen speeches; everybody
professes to hate speaking, and everybody secretly
wishes to get on his legs. But the undergraduate is
still at the stage of tolerable sincerity. He cherishes
a real conviction that to make a speech in public is
the same thing as to make a fool of yourself; he
assumes, at any rate, that an orator may be pre-

sumed to be a fool until he has proved the contrary.
And hence the real value of the Union. It tests a
man's possession of that most inestimable quality in
youth, a perfect willingness to make yourself ridiculous in public. There are, of course, two classes who
possess this power. There is the fool pure and
simple ; the man whose hide is too thick to feel the
lash ; who endures laughter out of sheer insensi-
bility, and who can, of course, only develope into the
genuine bore. But there is also the lad who is
impelled to talk nonsense by exuberant animal
spirits and youthful vanity; as soon as he is taken
out of the traces which bind him to the drudgery of
his studies, he flings up his heels and disports himself in the fields of rhetoric. Of course he talks
nonsense ; every one talks nonsense at twenty-one,
and mistakes it for the purest wisdom; but if it
comes plentifully and spontaneously, and with a
certain sparkle and effervescence promising better
things, it is merely a proof of a vivacious intellect.
I think there is no better sign of a certain originality
than this irresistible desire for display, where public
opinion gives such a ready excuse for dulness. It is

so very easy not to make a speech, because of course you are much too wise, that I respect a man who talks at the risk of looking silly.

I fear that our debates have lately been rather dull. We have no party battles to fight, such as raged during the Reform Bill or the Tractarian movement. We are in the condition which the Yankees call "spoiling for a fight." The Americans, indeed, have been kind enough to provide us with a little excitement, but I have heard of no very violent expressions of opinion. I believe that some one prayed for the day when grass might grow in the streets of New York, and the buffalo and the rattlesnake browse side by side on the heights of Bunker's Hill. The Opposition orator probably said that he should be content with nothing less than the complete and final extirpation of the Southern slaveholders.

But these amenities produced no real enthusiasm. I remember a far more exciting day, when the chartist ardour burnt in the bosoms of a small minority. An orator had worked himself to a pitch almost intolerable; he had pictured the priests seated on their

5—2

golden thrones and crunching between their teeth
(in a somewhat metaphorical sense) the flesh and
bones of the people; he had apostrophized the pure
and virtuous soul of Marat, and shocked our patriotism by praying for an army of French republicans
to re-enact Pride's Purge, and inoculate the British
populace with the true social virus. The Conservative majority of course groaned at his monstrosities
and cheered the next speaker, who, after describing
Louis Philippe as the wisest king who ever "sat
upon the crown of France," proceeded to denounce
his rebellious subjects. This was too much for our
radical leader, who unluckily took to brandishing a
decanter of water beyond the fair limits of parlia-
mentary gesticulation. The president put a motion
for his instant expulsion, which was carried by accla-
mation, and immediately enforced by a unanimous
charge from the overwhelming majority. The radicals defended for a moment a difficult angle in the
staircase, but were soon swept tumultuously into the
street amidst tremendous cheers. Those days have
passed; we have become decent, and scarcely even
get up a personal squabble. As the society is now

plunging into bricks and mortar, I live in reasonable hope that some difficulty may turn up ; a good dispute about private business is always amusing and does no one any harm.

Carlyle is fond of the aphorism, " Speech is silvern ; silence is golden." I confess that I have never been able even to guess what it means. If silver stands for speech and gold for silence, what does copper represent ? But, besides this, would it not be rather absurd to say that night is better than day, or sleep than waking, or that women are of more importance than men ? Of course Mr. Carlyle really wishes to say that most people talk too much ; he uses, in my opinion, a most illogical formula to express it ; however that may be, I entirely disagree with his sentiment as far as our students are concerned. I think that speech is a very desirable faculty for them to exercise, and that they would hardly get it exercised at all except in this voluntary arena. I resign myself to the non-sense, which is the inevitable result, without any regret, for so long as criticism is so hostile to speaking in general, there is no danger of the excessive production of the commodity.

VII.

VARIOUS.

IF I were giving a complete natural history of the genus undergraduate, I should still have many subvarieties to describe. I should have, for example, to depict the extreme High Churchman, of whom a few choice specimens still linger amongst us. Certain annual ceremonies plunge our townsmen into a frenzy, which seeks relief by denouncing the Scarlet Woman in the local journals. Not very long ago a youth opened an " oratory " in his rooms. For this pious purpose he selected his " gyp-room," a small apartment generally consecrated to pots and pans, decanters, and slop-pails. In it he erected an altar, decked with the due amount of candles and flowers, and opened it with a solemn procession, headed by certain weak-minded University officials. Of course, he was put down. Tomfoolery of this kind thrives ill in our soil. We prefer, of the two, the more manly, if less refined, evangelical fanaticism. Over-zealous youths preach open-air sermons, or invite the University at large to "prayer meetings conducted by undergraduates." I should be sorry to speak of these well-meant efforts, because I could not describe them in the simplest terms without making them ridiculous. They make but little impression, too, on the dogged common sense of the ordinary under-graduate. Their worst effect is that they lead him to class all rather eccentric religious manifestations under the head (I apologize for quoting his rather inelegant slang) of "awful bosh."

Nor am I going to speak of those who form in some sort the antipodes to these zealots, the young gentlemen whose talk is of horse-racing, or of betting, or of billiards. They are a mere faint reflection of the great outside sporting world, who have neither engrafted any special characteristics upon our little society, nor taken any strong colouring from their (sometimes very precarious) sojourn amongst us. Both in athletic sports and in study we flatter ourselves that we occasionally are at the head of English progress; in this department we are merely feeble imitators, and the model from which we copy may be studied in London or elsewhere.

I will conclude the subject of undergraduate manners and customs by touching shortly upon one or two further illustrations of their intellectual and social tendencies. Every one who has left the University for a few years looks back with special interest upon some of the pet amusements of the little set to which he belonged. He remembers the absorbing interest which he gave to the noble study of whist, or his occasional excursions into the more gambling mysteries of loo or vingt-un. He recollects the morning on which he startled the early dean on his way to chapel by the profane cry of "Bobs up!" proceeding from a belated card-party; or how, on escaping from the torments of a scholarship examination, he signalized his liberty by playing cards for twenty-four consecutive hours, declining gradually, as his intellect grew weak, from the intellectual strain of whist down to cutting through the pack for shillings. He remembers that glorious long vacation, when lectures were not and chapels were few : and when he met a few quiet friends for " a Shakspeare," when he was ready for every character, from Hamlet down to "a confused noise within," and finished the evening with a domestic rubber. Or, to go a step higher, he remembers the knot of youthful philosophers who met on Saturday evenings to discuss all problems in heaven or earth :—

> Where once we held debate, a band
> Of youthful friends, on mind, and art,
> And labour, and the changing mart,
> And all the framework of the land;

and, indeed, talked incredible nonsense on all those subjects. And yet few things probably did him more good than those rambling and not very orthodox discussions. He learnt to use the tools of his trade, and if his youthful confidence led him to solve a good many problems incapable of solution, it stimulated his powers, and prepared them for maturer struggles.

I well remember the awe with which I listened to a young logician, who declared himself to have discovered seventy-six new forms of syllogism, most of which, as he added, were inexpressible in human language, and, indeed, totally unthinkable by human faculties. I discovered for myself an ingenious system, which somehow combined the results of Locke and Hegel. It requires, indeed, either a very childish mind or the mind of a German philosopher (which comes to much the same thing) to study metaphysics with any expectation of coming to a useful result; but Sir W. Hamilton was doubtless right in vaunting its merit as a system of mental gymnastics, and I always thought it very wrong in Milton to consign the question of fate and free-will to diabolic disputants. The study is very pleasant, and requires a certain youthful confidence and buoyancy of spirit. If the tendency of our arguments would have occasionally shocked our parents and guardians, I don't think we were any the worse for them permanently : it is no bad preparation even for an orthodox theologian to have talked something verging upon infidelity in his youth; he will have learned the trick of it, and will at least remember the use of free speech and honest, though absurdly superficial, inquiry.

There is another kind of reminiscence of which a great deal is generally made in University novels. There is a type of hero, partially represented in *Guy Livingston*, the audacious youth who shows his spirit in getting drunk and fighting bargees. This variety of undergraduate in reality differs from his picture as much as the dirty drunken Red Indian of real life differs from the Red Indian of Fenimore Cooper's novels.

The town and gown row of practice is a singularly stupid affair. The fiction is beautifully caricatured in the model novel, where the youthful aristocrat is in danger of being thrashed by the gigantic bargee who " likes whopping a lord," till Raphael Mendoza descends into the ring, and gives 10,000*l.* to each of the bargee's ten children. In practice it is in this wise. A few undergraduates perambulate the streets; a number of dirty boys throw stones from behind corners. If one undergraduate is caught alone by half-a-dozen big ruffians, they sometimes thrash him and sometimes he runs away. The authorities send home every one they catch, and admonish a few next morning, when the affair terminates.

In former days, when manners were rougher and preserved something of the prize-fighting element, it was sometimes a more serious affair. A friend of mine has described to me his sensations as he lay on the ground with a big blackguard kneeling on his chest and remarking affably to a friend, " Wait till I get a stone to fettle his mouth with." In those days the police sometimes interfered on the side of the town, and another gentleman related how, as he was prostrate in the same fashion, a truncheon tapped him gradually along his backbone till it came to his head, after which he remembered nothing more, and was laid up for six months. We have changed all that; the most serious damage of which I heard on the last celebration of our Saturnalia, was caused by a young gentleman who descended into the streets, " flown," I presume, " with insolence and wine," and, in the dark, knocked down the first pugnacious man he met, receiving a black eye in return. On examination, it appeared that his adversary had descended with similar good intentions from the same wine-party.

And this may introduce a word or two on the

wine-bibbing, which is the other prominent idea of
the fast school of University novelists. It is an
undeniable fact that undergraduates occasionally get
drunk. Moreover, as I have before observed, when
they get drunk they do it with a will. But, as in
other classes of society, intoxication is rapidly becoming rarer and less respectable. I can remember
orgies, which would not now be tolerated, which rose
to the pitch of hurling tumblers at each other's heads :
one noisy gentleman was temporarily squelched by a
friend, who used a large bowl-full of milk-punch in
the guise of a helmet, pressing it well down over his
head and shoulders ; and they (I will not say we)
finished by hunting the soberest man of the party
with wild shrieks over the college grounds with the
expressed intention of putting him safely to bed.
He obstinately declined the proffered assistance.

The outbursts of hilarity that occasionally occur
grow less obnoxious ; and, such as they are, rather
tend to prove the general sobriety of the performers ;
for it is your habitually sober man who becomes un-
manageable and eccentric when he has imbibed too
much liquor. After a month's training for a boat-

race or an examination, some men persist in thinking
that they have a right to an evening's "enjoyment."
I remember a youth, distinguished rather on the river
than in examinations, who astonished us on such an
occasion by developing hitherto unknown faculties.
One Jones, remarkable chiefly for propriety in dress,
had invited him to celebrate one of his athletic
victories by the usual supper. At a late hour the
guest rose to return thanks. "Some men," he
began, with a drunken affectation of wisdom, "have
both brains and muscles," pointing with a graceful
bow to a neighbour; "some have no muscles,
but brains, like Smith"—Smith being a diminutive
but highly sagacious coxwain; — "some have no
brains, but muscles, like me; and some," turning
suddenly upon our host, "have no brains nor muscles,
but collars, like Jones."

I fear that my friend's sermons have not sustained
the reputation for eloquence which he won by this
brilliant apostrophe. After the speech he had a dim
impression of having insulted some one, and naturally
assumed that it was his college tutor. Accordingly,
he put on his cap, gown, surplice, and great-coat, by

way of academical uniform, and taking a moderator-
lamp in his hand, rushed into the court to make an
apology. We succeeded in steering him into the
back-garden, where he peacefully fell asleep under
a tree.

The intoxicated undergraduate is generally beset
by this shadowy idea, that he either has insulted,
or immediately ought to insult, the college authorities. It was beautifully illustrated by a pupil of his
whom my friend Brown discovered clinging desperately to a tree and trying to drive a corkscrew into
the bark. "What on earth are you about?" he
inquired. "I'm screwing up that old fool, Brown,
into his room," was the touching reply.

As a rule, I am happy to say that in this, as in
other respects, I have witnessed a very great improvement in our University morality. Anything approaching to habitual intoxication is all but unknown.
Entertainments tend, on the whole, to become more
rational. A few academical generations back it was
the custom to indulge in horrid celebrations called
"wines." Twenty or thirty youths collected together
to a heavy dessert, washed down by execrable fluids.

These dismal gatherings are going out of fashion. I may here put in one word for the much-abused weed, tobacco. I daresay it ruins the constitution of every smoker, though my own is hitherto in tolerable order; but it certainly tends to discourage the consumption of the fluid known as wine in university towns.

Before dismissing the consideration of undergraduate life, let me say a word or two on its general aspect. I have given my opinion of our education, of our sports, and of our more irregular and unsystematic influences. The general result seems to me to be satisfactory. It has been said that the ideal of the German student is to be a man, and that of the English student to be a gentleman. It is intended to imply that the German is a superior being, and that the Englishman is tainted by a certain snobbishness, and a preference of superficial elegance to thorough work. I do not wish to compare the net result. The German has, doubtless, his advantages. When he is not a mere beer-barrel, or a mere receiver of a tobacco-pipe, or a mere piece of intellectual machinery for grinding metaphysics or natural philosophy, he is doubtless an amiable and excellent creature. But I think it must be admitted that the Englishman's ideal includes one or two manly qualities. Notwithstanding all the nonsense that has been poured out about athletic virtues, there is still some residue of sense at the bottom of it. No one who saw the late University race, or the athletic sports, will deny that our lads possess some good physical stuff which it would be hard to match elsewhere. When German "turners" or French students will do the like I shall have a higher opinion of them.

Meanwhile, though Mr. Arnold sneers at us for calling ourselves "the best breed in the universe," I don't think there are many better. And I have endeavoured to show that we carry into our intellectual pursuits much of the same tough, indomitable vigour that every one can see exhibited in bone and muscle. We don't turn out many very learned men —the temptations to practical life in England are too overpowering ; but we turn out plenty of hard-headed, energetic men, fit to fight a good battle in the world. We turn out also a good many grossly ignorant lads, without any education to speak of. That will doubtless

6

be improved, and even they are not deficient in some really great qualities. However that may be, I should think the worse of any one who had passed as many years as I have done in a University town without learning to sympathize with and to admire the high-spirited and vigorous lads who take many of their most enduring impressions from their three or four years of study within our walls.

VIII.

DONS.

I AM now approaching a more delicate part of my task. Hitherto I have attempted to sketch a few phases of undergraduate life, and undergraduates are, after all, nothing but a body of young Englishmen of the average type, not very profoundly affected by the influences of the place. Those influences have not had time to produce, as it were, a chemical effect upon their mental constitution; they only coat it with a superficial deposit. The youth often takes off with his cap and gown all that divides him from the common herd of mankind. He becomes, as Falstaff says, little better than one of the wicked. A few associations drawn from the river, the cricket-field,

or the lecture-room still float in his mind. He pre-
serves, possibly even for life, some college friend-
ships. He carries away more or less intellectual
and social polish. But without depreciating the
benefits of a University education, I must confess
that in three years we cannot change our geese
into swans ; we must be content with giving to our
goslings a rather more graceful gait.

It is very different with those who have passed
the best years of their lives within our walls, who
have imbibed our prejudices and our creeds with
their daily food, and who have, as it were, taken the
very shape of the walls within which they live. The
toad of country newspapers, which probably sported
in the waters where Adam bathed his sturdy limbs
(I believe that to be the correct expression), and has
passed the intervening years in a block of coal, is
moulded by the ins and outs of his own particular
cranny. It may be improper to draw an elaborate
parallel between toads and dons, further than to
remark that with an unpromising exterior they both
sometimes bear a precious jewel in their heads ;
but I certainly never hear of the toad whose toes

have grown long and whose mouth has been closed
by a prolonged sojourn in the rock without thinking
of some of my University friends. They, like the
toad, have absorbed a certain local colouring; some
of their faculties have become cramped from long
disuse; and as the shape of the toad's domicile
might be inferred from an inspection of his person,
so I fancy that I can distinguish in some men not
only the University but even the particular college
to which they have belonged. In one figure I can
distinctly trace the marks left by a chapel of pure
mediæval architecture; in another I can make out
the influence of a lawn admirably adapted for croquet; and, without being hypercritical, the contour
of a third speaks to me with irresistible force of a
certain excellent college kitchen and cellar.

It would doubtless require much practice and
local knowledge to distinguish with any certainty
the minute péculiarities of a stamp impressed upon
such varying raw material. To the outside world a
member of Trinity Hall may resemble a Caius man,
and even an Oxford don (incredible as it appears to
me) resemble one from Cambridge. The skilful

observer distinguishes the members of different colleges as a shepherd knows one sheep of his flock from another, and the members of different Universities as the shepherd tells the sheep from the goats. The interval which separates both classes from the outside world must be paralleled by the division between sheep and swine. Of course I am not so illiberal as (openly) to compare Oxford men to the goats, or the outside world to pigs. I speak only of the profundity of the distinction, not of its special nature.

There should, therefore, be no difficulty in describing the prominent peculiarities of so strongly marked a class, although I must add that there is some delicacy in describing peculiarities which you may be supposed yourself to share. To see ourselves as others see us is a gift to be devoutly prayed for, or, in other words, to be rarely obtained. When you have only to glance at the looking-glass for the original of your portrait, the lines are somehow apt to become distorted. Those, however, who have painted us from the outside have perpetrated what seem to me such gross caricatures as to justify

me in endeavouring to supply some of their defi-
ciencies. Two or three wretched dummies with a
strong family likeness are generally made to do duty
for the don of fiction. A " don " has indeed become
a proverbial expression for an unpleasant variety of
the great genus prig. He was portrayed with inimitable skill by Mr. Thackeray in the *Snob Papers*.

Small variations on the same tune have been
played by every variety of humbler novelist, till we
have become a byword and a scorn. We are
supposed to be walking bags of dry bones, given to
snubbing generous young men, and regarding young
women with a strange mixture of awe and contempt.
I do not wonder at this in inferior novelists. They
are apt to classify all mankind according to their
varying relations to matrimony. As our relation is,
or has till lately been, of a purely negative character,
we are naturally regarded with special abhorrence.
We are considered as mere human ciphers, or as
professional bachelors supporting each other in a
creed of cynical indifference.

Sometimes one of us is described as being gallantly cut out from under the batteries of common-

room contempt by a female privateer ; or as emerging
into the broad daylight of the world in a dazzled and
owl-like condition, to remain for the rest of his life
in the condition of a half-civilized barbarian.   There
is a description of one favourite variety of this
fictitious don in the *Chronicles of Carlingford*.   The
victim of University life is supposed to take a college
living after an eighteen years' engagement, and to
find that neither he nor his wife can talk the proper
twaddle to old women in the country—an awful proof,
of course, of spiritual stagnation.   In another novel,
a gentleman whose hero has the chance of a Fellowship (I think) at Trinity, makes him spurn the offer
with becoming scorn, because he intends to marry,
and entertains the pleasing belief that wherever
Providence brings mouths into the world it will find
wherewithal to feed them.   The profane form of
this theory, by the way, is that you ought to marry
because your relations can't let you starve.   A good
many young clergymen appear to act upon one form
or other of the doctrine.   In Cambridge we don't
believe it ; partly, perhaps, because we have a
professor of political economy.   I cannot, however,

admit, as at present advised, that all bachelors are beyond the pale of human sympathy, nor that we are a particularly degraded class, even amongst bachelors.

It seems generally agreed by our critics that we are strange monastic beings who ought to be sent back to live in the middle ages. But it is well known that, at least in the popular creed, there are two varieties of monks. There is the monasticism at which Father Ignatius is playing with such childish delight, which involves a diet of the locust and wild-honey order, with raiment of camel's hair. Some rosy-cheeked don occasionally advocates this way of living after a good dinner in hall; but he is not supposed to find many followers, except amongst men training for the University boat, who have to come down a pound or two in weight.

The opposite variety of monk, who is described in the words of the poet as laughing ha, ha! and quaffing ha, ha! to an unlimited extent, is considered to be more liberally represented amongst us. I will not deny that there is some superficial verisimilitude about this. There are certain ceremonies, which we observe rather out of respect to our founders' wills than from any over-development of conviviality, which delude a temporary visitor into an undue estimate of our festivities.

Of course, too, we wish to be hospitable. A friend staying with me at Christmas (the period at which our college is in duty bound to consume the proceeds of a certain estate left some 300 years ago to provide "a moderate supper" for the fellows and scholars), after a heavy breakfast, which he is expected to wash down with beer, a luncheon interpolated between breakfast and five or six o'clock dinner, and a dinner which I hope is satisfactory, sometimes remarks (on being invited to conclude by a supper off boar's-head and game-pie, with a liquid compound whose recipe has been handed down through a long line of butlers from the middle ages,) that he could not do that kind of thing every day. He is evidently under the impression that I never dine without passing a grace-cup down the long hall table, and drinking *in piam memoriam fundatricis*, that I pass every morning in smoking cigars, drinking beer, and lounging about in my friends' rooms. As for the amount of daily eating and drinking which he imputes to me, I tremble to think of it.

He is apt to fortify this theory by another class of observations. I have met him one summer on the top of Mont Blanc, and another time in the Piræus or the Golden Horn; he knows that I have visited the banks of the Mississippi, inspected Moscow and the scene of the Polish insurrection, and passed a few winter vacations at Rome. On inquiring how I find time for this, he is informed that term time occupies five months in the year, and consequently the vacations seven months. If I do lead a monastic life, it must, he thinks, be one with certain alleviations; the severity of my intellectual exertions finds an appropriate relief in social relaxation; and seven-twelfths of my whole time may, if I choose, be spent as far from Cambridge as railroads and steamboats can carry me.

Of course it is easy to confute such a scoffer by pointing to the work actually done; the number of young men whose minds are cleared up as to the common pump and the lever, the number who are taught the eleven allegations which establish the truth of the Scriptures, and the number who are put through a severe training for honours, prove of course that their teachers are tolerably laborious,— a proposition which is still more conclusively established by the flood of light which is constantly being directed from Cambridge upon theology, mathematics, natural philosophy, and every branch of literature. The sun of England would probably set for ever, in an intellectual point of view, if our light were quenched. I will presently explain a little more fully the means by which such great results are obtained, and discriminate the various classes of workers in our busy hive.

Meanwhile, I am content with remarking that the various portraits of the don that I have mentioned are only the results of looking at a very diversified landscape from different points of view. By putting them all together, the true don will start up into stereoscopic reality. He is a man given to severe intellectual labour, familiar with Sanscrit or mysterious mathematics, or capable of unravelling chemical problems whose very terms are beyond any ordinary knowledge.

He passes his nights in original study, and his days in communicating his hard-won information to ingenuous youth. By them he is looked up to as a guide, philosopher, and friend; he condescends to direct even their athletic sports, and to lead them upwards into the highest regions of science. On occasions he can break out into a little graceful conviviality, where the coarse indulgence of appetite is qualified and corrected by old traditional observances; the grace-cup and the commemoration service sanctify his feastings. Nor is he entirely immured in his cloister; during the vacations, wisely lengthened to a considerable part of the year, he is able to enlarge his mind by foreign travel; and men may be met at Cambridge familiar with every quarter of the globe.

If such a man has been the victim of false caricature, he may remember that neither the greatest nor the best of men are entirely safe. Washington, Socrates, and the late Duke of Wellington were all unjustly lampooned, and why should he escape the common fate? True, he has been cruelly taunted with his enforced deprivation

of female society. If a good Conservative, he will
reply, "So much the better; women would break
up many of our social habits and split the strong
corporate feeling which holds us together. Why
should not one place in England be free from
female influence, or, in other words, from jobbery,
corruption, and discord?" If a Liberal, he will
say that we are improving. The married Fellow
—a few years ago as strange a monster as a
hippogriff—already swarms in our courts; we have
begun to examine girls, and the prophetic eye can
already see young lady undergraduates looming in
the distance of futurity.

IX.

TUITION.

ONE great difficulty of natural historians is to classify the subject of their labours on any satisfactory principles; and in endeavouring to depict, however slightly, the great genus Don, I find myself somewhat perplexed to arrange it in systematic order. As, however, it is not my purpose to attempt an exhaustive account of its peculiarities, I will content myself with one very simple but important distinction.

Mankind may be roughly divided here, as elsewhere, into the useful and the ornamental; it is our particular happiness that, although we have some who are included under both these heads, there are none who do not fall under one of them. Those who are of no assignable use whatever are of so highly ornamental a character, that I almost feel disposed to worship them. My state of mind in regard to a Master resembles that of a small boy of my acquaintance, in whose family lived a gorgeous coachman of noble appearance, and distinguished by one of those wigs which suggested to Sydney Smith, "a boundless convexity of frizz:" the boy was one night seen on his knees and overheard to pray, "Good Mr. Brown, watch over us this night!" When I was a small boy myself, it used to be pointed out to me that there was a kind of providential arrangement about these matters: the humble hen and the domestic sheep were plain, not to say ugly; whereas the vain peacock and mischievous tiger possessed a singular beauty. An unpleasant moral used to be drawn for my own private edification. Although I have since seen some reasons for doubting the precise accuracy both of the facts and of the interpretation put upon them, I have found a better illustration of the same principles within our walls. My weak imagination fails to conceive a more majestic and

imposing position than that of the Head of a House ;
I always envy those fortunate Masters of Arts who
have the happiness to precede him during his term
of office as Vice-Chancellor, bearing silver maces.
Some of the dignity which inspires every attitude,
and seems to surround his brow with a heavenly
aureole, must be communicated even to them—
ordinary mortals of our common clay. It is true
that I have also, after long and painful researches,
never been able to discover that the usefulness of a
Head of a House generally held any proportion to
his ornamental character. But I would say with
Tennyson, if I ventured to speak familiarly to these
noble creatures,

> Go look in any glass, and say
> What moral is in being fair?

Do we criticise a peacock's tail because we cannot
discover the object which it serves ? or would any
reasonable human being complain of the Nelson
column because it isn't a lamp-post ? If the Heads
are visible symbols of the beauty, dignity, and moral
and intellectual worth of the University, should not
that satisfy rash sceptics ? Is it not desirable that

7

some remnants should be left of that magnificent system of sinecures which so attracted the admiration of our forefathers ?

But I must, for the present, tear myself away from the contemplation of these noble objects, to describe the humbler and more useful mortals who carry on what is popularly supposed to be the chief object of our Universities—the instruction of youth.

There are various subdivisions amongst these, according to the degree in which our instructors partake of the splendours and the uselessness of an official position. Highest in the scale come the professors, whose labours in teaching are distinctly perceptible by the naked eye ; below them are the college tutors, whose teaching would perhaps be more effective if they were not distracted by the awful responsibility of keeping their pupils out of scrapes ; and in the lowest place are the private tutors, " coaches," according to the established slang, who do perhaps two-thirds of the actual work of instruction.

To my mind, one of the most miserable positions in this world is that of a schoolmaster. Some people,

I know, like it, just as there are some people who like
feeding pigs, or drawing teeth, or any other useful
but generally obnoxious occupation.   Boys are,
perhaps, the most detestable objects in creation—
worse than monkeys in so far as they are better
imitations of men; and to live surrounded by a
swarm of boys, responsible for their feeding, washing,
and education, bearing the taunts and grumblings of
outrageous parents, seems to me as wretched a fate
as to live in a wasp's nest.

Next above schoolmasters in the scale of misery,
I should place what we call a " poll coach;" the
unfortunate being who undertakes to steer the help-
less undergraduate through the shoals and quicksands
of the poll degree. He has to deal with human
beings who are less restless and more doggedly indifferent than boys; with a trust and reverence which
is really touching, they implicitly abandon all charge
of their own thoughts, and surrender their minds
to him as passive vessels to be pumped into. They
only hope that he will pump in as little as possible,
in order that they may discharge it the more readily.
To do such a duty thoroughly well demands two

qualifications : a perfect temper and a qualified omniscience ; a man's knowledge, that is, must extend over the whole field of University requirements, but need never penetrate below the surface.

The rooms in which the trade is carried on give you some picture of the occupant's mind. A huge sheet of paper pinned against a wall contains the evidence of the Christian religion reduced, like portable soup, to a small compass. It is to be hoped that it is not used as stock for making sermons. Two or three mechanical toys stand upon the table ; for the poll man, having a general impression that a thing in a book corresponds to nothing in earth or heaven (the last is specially unlikely), shows an almost infantile delight at the sight of a real pulley or inclined plane. The one-ounce weight, it is true, does not accurately balance the six, as the book says it should ; but the " coach" has judiciously secured equilibrium by inserting a surreptitious pin into the mechanism. Certain manuscript books on the table contain the results of boiling down human knowledge into shreds and patches, for the " poll coach" is ready to prepare his pupils for any known pass examination; if they gave him a day's start to learn it, he will teach them Sanskrit, Chaldee, or German metaphysics.

You find, therefore, mechanical propositions written in the fewest possible words, lists of the early heretics and their tenets, a short account of the Reformation, a statement of the four causes which make the division of labour desirable, and of the three causes of the economical disadvantages of slavery, pet translations of classical fragments, with marks against noted pitfalls, a short history of the German tribes, &c., besides various other information at which my knowledge does not enable me even to hint.

It is bad enough to have to acquire this information, but a man requires the temper of an angel to stand cross-questioning about all parts of it at random from sixty or seventy distracting youths from eight in the morning to any time at night. Like other artists, however, the " poll coach" learns to take a pride in his work. He looks upon a refractory youth with the feelings of a Rarey regarding Cruiser. The poll youth is shy of any instructor,

much as that redoubtable beast had an aversion
for grooms. He considers them as curious pieces
of mechanism, standing in some unknown relation
to a whip and a bit and bridle. The victim has
therefore to be tempted into the lecture-room by
gentle means: to be tempted even by occasional
indulgence in beer or tobacco in a retired part of
the establishment; when he makes a frantic plunge
and gives up study altogether, the tempting must
be repeated. When tolerably tamed, he still requires
incessant attention; the great difficulty of those
whom destiny has marked for plucking is that they
can neither keep their minds to one subject nor their
bodies in one place. They are incapable of steady
attention or steady habits. The object of the coach
is first to fix them down in his workshop, and then
to go through the exhausting process of assiduously
hammering knowledge into a fool. The most dis-
tressing case is when a man's mind is so constructed
as to contain five subjects at once, but not six. I
have known a youth of this kind who was plucked
seven times for his Little Go, and every time plucked
in only one subject. Once he succeeded in every-

thing but Euclid, another time he got up his Euclid and forgot his Scripture history; a third time he managed both of these, but failed in his Greek Testament. He was like a child trying to pick up six marbles when its hand was only big enough to hold five.

Driving refractory pigs always wanting to stand still or to bolt in the wrong direction is known to be trying to the temper. " Pigs is awkward animals to drive—specially when there's many of them—very," according to Thucydides; and the same observation applies to the equally refractory and lazy animal called a poll man. I once tried my hand at the work; but happening to describe some men who were chattering round me in a senseless manner, as a " set of gibbering maniacs," I found that they did not like it. I have ever since respected the men who can go on from year to year, all day long and almost every day, in vacation and term time, carrying on this most irritating occupation without learning to hate and despise their species. I saw a statement the other day, that when Dr. Dodd had broken down in preaching, tuition, and every other employment except forging, he "descended so low as to become the editor of a newspaper." I am not certain that I would not have tried this climax of degradation before the tuition. I would rather be tormented even by contributors, vexatious as they must be, than by pupils.

Teaching of course improves as an employment, with the improvement of the raw material. It is pleasanter to teach a clever man than a stupid one, or rather it is not so exquisitely disagreeable, for even the highest branches of the art have troubles of their own. The thorough idiot wants to be kept up to his work, gently but firmly; if he doesn't understand a thing you say, "Learn it by heart;" if he forgets it you say, "Learn it again," and so on until seventy times seven. The clever youth goes through a routine equally vexatious after a little experience. I remember the time when a burst of military ardour led me to display my portly form in the becoming uniform of the University Rifle Corps. That stately person the serjeant-major must, I fancy, have had a poor time of it. The first thousand times or so that he explained to us the correct way of forming fours,

I daresay he put a little intellect into it ; he attached some sort of meaning to the stream of gibberish which flowed so glibly from his lips. But about the thousand and first time it must have become tiresome ; he must have done it as instinctively as a Prime Minister telling a deputation that her Majesty's Government will give their best consideration to its requests, or a toll-collector giving you change for a penny, or an orthodox parson telling you that Colenso is a shallow copyist.

Now, it is much the same in teaching an intelligent youth the differential calculus, or explaining a corrupt passage in a classical author to him. You know the exact point at which he will begin to look stupid ; you foresee the look of partial intelligence with which he will receive your well-worn explanation, and the stupid remark a little further on which will show that he failed to see the point of it. The ancients would not have condemned Sisyphus to roll a stone up a hill if they had been a little wiser ; they would have set him to explain Euclid's proof of the forty-seventh proposition to a series of Bœotian students.

I believe, however, that this is not a philosophical view. We always pity the blind horse wearing his everlasting round in the mill. But he is said to be happy, and to cherish the delusion that he is really making progress in some direction. And I must confess than an impartial observation of this most useful and hardworking class proves them to be happy. Either the monotony of the employment acts as a sedative, or a man must have had a constitution superior to all irritability to be able to carry it on at all. I can see the placid and benevolent face of my old instructor now, and listen to his invariable exhortation "push on;" just as if I had been, as indeed I was, a wearied and disgusted wayfarer. Every morning he appeared in chapel punctually at 7.30. From 8 to 8.15 breakfast. Pupils from 8.15 to 3. Then a constitutional so regular, that we used to believe that the philosophers at the observatory took their time from the instant at which he passed the gates, instead of remarking the sun's transit, which indeed is apt to be invisible in our misty climate. At 4 dinner. From 5.30 to 10 pupils again, with ten minutes' interval for refreshment.

He lived in a perfect atmosphere of mathematics; his books, all ranged in the neatest order, and covered with uniform brown paper, were mathematical; his talk, to us at any rate, was one round of mathematics: even his chairs and tables, strictly limited to the requirements of pupils, and the pattern on his carpet, seemed to breathe mathematics. By what mysterious process it was that he accumulated stores of miscellaneous information and knew all about the events of the time (for such I afterwards discovered to be the fact), I have never been able to guess. Probably he imbibed them through the pores of his skin. Still less can I imagine how it came to pass that he published a whole series of excellent educational works. He probably wrote them in momentary interstices of time, between one pupil's entering his sanctum and another leaving it. Such, however, is the life of some of our hardworking men, and they seem to enjoy it.

X.

COLLEGE TUTORS.

THE private tutors, of whom I have just spoken, do a considerable part of the work of tuition ; but they are, in an official point of view, mere excrescences upon our system. They are rather volunteers than soldiers in the regular organized army. The college *esprit de corps*, which is the mainspring of an English University, centres round the master, fellows, and scholars of those learned and religious foundations for which, " as in private duty bound," our preachers weekly entreat our prayers. Without the colleges the University would sink to the level of the institution profanely known (I never could guess why) as Stincomalee. We love the University as an American loves the Union, with a reflective passion bred rather in the head than in the heart; for our college we feel the warm personal enthusiasm that the Southern planter bears to South Carolina or the "old dominion." Patriotism is sometimes warmer and less intelligent, as its object becomes more limited. A general is said to have bid his troops "remember that they were Portuguese" (not, one would have thought, a very stirring reminiscence); an inhabitant of Jersey considers that the chief jewel in the British crown is represented by the Channel Islands; and, on the same principle, every undergraduate always assumes that the members of his own college are a special breed of men, possessing an amount of pluck, good manners, and good feeling unknown elsewhere. He holds this faith simply, without attempting to account for the mysterious dispensation of Providence, which has directed so much virtue and talent to his little society; and speaks of "out college men" with that pleasant contempt which Englishmen habitually express for foreigners and natives in general.

The maintenance of this spirit, which is at least

a useful stimulus to exertion, and forms many pleasant bonds of friendship, depends to a great extent upon the college authorities, and especially upon the tutors. In all armies, the influence of the commander's character is important, even when unperceived. The undergraduate is probably ignorant of the value of the gentleman whom he stigmatizes as a "duffer" (the modern slang for the antiquated term "muff"), and describes in private as "old Stick-in-the-mud." With the thoughtlessness of youth he attacks the very qualities by which he is most benefited. That which chiefly irritates him is one which we all learn to admire as we grow older, and which is to be found in its highest purity in some college tutors—I mean a spotless respectability.

It would be worth while for a social philosopher to analyse and describe the ingredients which go to make up this character. The test suggested in the trial of Thurtell, that a respectable man was one who kept a gig, is obviously adapted to a ruder state of society. I am inclined, after some meditation, to suggest as a preferable one for modern use, the power of wearing the black (or "chimney pot") hat of the period on all occasions without manifest incongruity. It occurred to me one sunny afternoon when I was (I must confess) smoking a pipe in an old coat and a six weeks' beard on the steps of an inn in a remote Swiss village. A black hat and a white tie, forming the framework of a clean-shaven face, suddenly dawned upon me, and their owner inquired where English Divine service was held? I had just enough presence of mind left to direct him to a roomful of German students and to retire hastily.

A man who can live up to a black hat in an Alpine tour is equal to any position in life. Thackeray tells us of the unlucky clerk who was ruined by having to bring himself into harmony with a diamond ring. To live each day so that a black hat may not jar upon the sense of congruity of lookers-on almost amounts to putting yourself in training for a bishopric. Now the cap and gown of the University don are to the hat what the hat is to the wideawake or Scotch bonnet. No human being could wear them all the year round; long vacations are mercifully interposed to enable us to bear the weight of our own splendour. We come

back revived from contact with common men, just
as a distinguished writer in the last century used
to refresh himself after a conversation with philosophers and poets by smoking a pipe at the bar of
a low public-house.

The advantages which a tutor gains by living in
a state of what Eöthen calls " utter respectability,"
may not be at once obvious. I must remark, therefore, that all kinds of schoolmasters, amongst whom
I venture to class this their noblest variety, as Professor Huxley classes man with the gorilla, have two
sorts of subjects to keep in order—namely, pupils
and parents. Now, although the tutor is far above
the vanity of tempting parents to confide their sons
to his care, and, indeed, only accepts the charge as
an act of condescending favour, he ought to exert
a magnetic influence over them. Without soliciting
their favour, he should attract them by an imper-
ceptible power. They should come to him as moths
come to the candle, with an instinctive confidence.
Nothing is found more attractive in this way than
that indefinable aura of respectability which surrounds
some men like an atmosphere, and causes you to be

sensible of their presence even before your coarser senses have given you warning of their approach.

I am residing, we will suppose, in some remote country town. I take up the local paper and remark that Mr. A. B., the distinguished fellow and tutor of so-and-so, has been attending the consecration of the new church by the bishop of the diocese. Further on, I observe that Mr. A. B., as University Syndic (a name of vague but almost overpowering import) has been making some telling remarks about middle-class examinations. In another paragraph, the distinguished fellow and tutor has been distributing prizes to a school, and accompanied his distribution with some observations of startling novelty upon the importance of youthful industry. What can be more natural than that I should fly to confide my youthful son to his charge? The parent thus impelled is ushered into the tutor's rooms. This parent, as my tutorial friends inform me, is an animal of fidgety and easily startled disposition. A cigar-box or a hunting-whip carelessly left about might give a hopeless shock to his nerves. Once fascinated by the genuine tutor, however, he has no more chance than a bluebottle in a spider's web. His son, in nine cases out of ten, is a youth whose peculiar constitution renders hard work undesirable ; his mother has sent careful messages to be delivered as to the airing of his sheets and the dangers of over-exertion on the river or in the lecture-room. The parent endeavours to remember them.

Meanwhile engravings after the old masters look down upon him with placid contempt from the walls. The range of chapel windows is conspicuous through mullioned windows in the background. Classical authors and a copy of a sermon preached to the college audience rest in dignified repose on the table. Even the chairs and tables of Gothic design are suggestive of studious mediæval leisure. And these surroundings fit the accomplished tutor as naturally as a tortoise is fitted by his shell. It need hardly be said that the son is entered, that the parental requests die away upon his lips, and that he is, in fact, tamed as completely as Rarey tamed Cruiser. When he gets back to his country parish he may speak complacently of his visit to his old University and his dinner in the college hall ; but he will never venture to cavil at items in a college bill, or to complain of the tutor when his son is plucked, or to perform any of the vagaries which render ill-regulated parents obnoxious to the tutorial mind. In former days a strong Evangelical tendency was a useful adjunct to these great means for attracting and suppressing the parent. I should say that at present the best theological mixture was a good safe orthodoxy, strongly opposed to *Essays and Reviews,* but opposed with equal decision to any less noxious eccentricities.

The raw youth is, perhaps, harder to bring into thorough subjection. There is an entry in the books of one of our colleges, of a lad who came up to enter upon his studies; *sed, Euclide viso,* it emphatically adds, *cohorruit et evasit.* Such premature boltings on the sight of the implements of instruction are not perhaps common, but the recalcitrant spirit, of which this youth gave such an eminent example, remains and requires to be quelled.

No tutor is a hero to his pupils; they exaggerate his weaknesses with unpleasant acuteness, retail small stories of traditional blunders, and represent

8—2

themselves as treating him with an affable contempt. An undergraduate once informed me that he had been summoned to the dean one morning on account of repeated absence from chapel.   He made the ingenious excuse that there was a temporary tightness in one of his boots.   The dean, becoming inquisitive a few days later, was informed that the tightness still continued; and, on venturing a third remonstrance, was told that the tightness had produced an abrasion, which would require some days to heal.   In short, the authority was represented as a feeble creature, who could always be either bullied or bamboozled.

The facts of my friend's story were probably slightly distorted.   He had most likely shifted from one leg to another in the dean's room, making inarticulate noises for a quarter of an hour.   He had faintly alleged inflammation of the lungs, a severe heart disease, and various other excuses, till a skilful cross-examination had driven him to take refuge (metaphorically speaking) in his boots.

The struggle, however, between dignity and impudence is sometimes severe and protracted, and it is only by degrees that the supremacy of intense respectability asserts itself. When the noise of the untimely cornopean is hushed in the courts, when the grass-plots are left untrampled, when a lively fire is not kept up with saloon pistols at the notices fixed on the chapel door, when supper-parties retire home in peace instead of playing bowls in the quadrangle with the college plates and glasses, when chapels and lectures are regularly attended, and, as a natural consequence, the number of plucks falls off to nothing, the tutor may feel that he, like Van Amburgh, has reduced his menagerie to order. He has shown a dignity befitting a loftier position; with the help of a commentary on an epistle, or an essay to distil logical Christianity out of atheism, he may soar towards the con-genial atmosphere of the bishop's bench; there, the magnificent repose of manner which once humbled the most unruly undergraduate, may terrify the country clergy, and overawe curates of extravagant tendencies.

There are, of course, other ways besides that I have pointed out, in which a tutor may successfully sway the rod of empire. For example, he may go beyond the ordinary routine of lectures and endeavour to teach his pupils something. He may take a pride in the number of first-classes or wranglers that he can manufacture out of indifferent raw material, or a humbler pleasure in the number he can save from actual plucking. The objections to this course are, however, obvious. In the first place, it takes much time and trouble, for which he receives no extra pay, and even in a model University, we can't rely exclusively upon unselfish motives of action.

Again, a college tutor, whose mind is incessantly distracted by the cares of office, by corresponding with parents, maintaining discipline, and a hundred vexatious details, cannot, as a rule, successfully compete with the private tutor. And, finally, if the tutor considers himself, as he of course should, as the caterpillar which is to be developed into the butterfly dignity of a bishop, a head of a house, or, at lowest, a divinity professor, the drudgery of teaching prevents him from studying the full graces of his character. He can have no time to appear in the University pulpit, or to throw off those elegant theological works which I have recommended to his notice.

There are other and lower expedients which the tutor may adopt. He may affect to be on terms of familiarity with his pupils, join in their athletic games, and win glory by coaching the college crew. Of such a one a story is told illustrating his performance in a Greek Testament lecture. " Hallo ! " he is said to have exclaimed, " easy all ! Hard word there. Smith, what does it mean ? "

" I don't know," says Smith.

" No more don't I," replied the aquatic, but moderately learned, tutor ; " paddle on all ! "

The anecdote is probably not true, or I would not repeat it, but it is doubtless founded on fact.

I might go further yet by quoting legends from former ages. In the days when three-bottle men still existed and cockfighting was fashionable, there were tutors who affected the reverse of respectability. They affably got drunk at undergraduates' supper-parties ; one of them, it is said, issued from his college gates late at night, and smote the first man he met on the head with a poker, insomuch that his life was despaired of for six weeks ; the master of the college, however, took severe notice of this delinquent by insisting upon his accepting a small college living which happened to be vacant. The deeds of another tutor may be guessed from the story that he refused to move the college pump into a more convenient position, because, where it was, it enabled the under-graduates to get over the wall at night.

Such things, of course, have been unknown for the last half-century. Respectability has spread its leaden mantle over the whole country, the old eccentric characters have died out from our walls, and the man wins the race who can worship that great goddess with the most undivided devotion.

XI.

HEADS OF HOUSES.

At a very early period of my infancy, I proposed, in common with others of my cotemporaries, to rival the late Duke of Wellington or Admiral Nelson. At a subsequent epoch I came to the conclusion that on the whole it would be more feasible to become a second Sir Walter Scott. I even got so far as to compose a poem in pursuance of this design. The subject was the " Prairie on Fire," the only verses which I can at present remember being—

> See the bisons in despair,
> How they tear their grizzly hair,

or words to that effect. A difficulty in ensuring a sufficient supply of rhymes caused me to abandon this ambition.

The next object that I proposed to myself was to become Lord Chancellor, and I often regret that the temptation of a college office induced me to abandon my chance of a post which I fancy I could have filled with some credit to myself and with decided advantage to my relatives.

I then resolved upon becoming a bishop; I had little doubts of success, especially after the temporary return to the University of a gentleman who had succeeded in reaching that desirable goal of ambition. He said, or was said to have said, that nothing was easier than to gain a bishopric if you were only " up to snuff "—a slang expression which nothing but episcopal authority would have emboldened me to quote. There is, I believe, some truth in the saying, and I have long meditated a work on the art of becoming a bishop. I should lay down the precise theological shade which it is desirable to adopt; the books to publish, including a discussion of the rival merits of a commentary on the Gospels, an edition of a classical author, and an essay on Christian logic; the best means of advertising your merits, as by preaching University sermons, or becoming a noted "man of business"—and so forth. My enthusiasm was, however, somewhat quenched by considering the manifest inadequacy of the salary. In the good old times, when a bishop might have possibly got his twenty thousand a year and done nothing for it, there was much to be said for the office. Now that a paltry five thousand has to be set against the burdens of a palace, episcopal hospitality, and a steady discharge of all kinds of business duties, it can scarcely be said to be worth acceptance.

I therefore made a fresh survey of the field of human ambition, and came decidedly to the conclusion that, on the whole, few offices are really preferable in solid advantages to the headship of a college. You are not, it is true, in so conspicuous a position as some of those which I have mentioned; but you live in a picturesque old house, haunted by the associations of centuries. You succeed to a long line of dignitaries, interrupted half-way by the vulgar intrusion of the civil wars. In your own little world, you hold indisputably the first place. No one ever meets you who has a right to take precedence of you. You have a sufficient salary, and last, not least, you have nothing in the world to do. You have obtained an office which is a reward for past labours, or perhaps for past good fortune, and which imposes no future labour upon you. I say that it is or may be a reward for past good fortune, and this indeed is one of its special merits. A legend, which I believe to be well founded, tells how the mastership of a certain college was conferred in this wise: The fellows nominated two persons of certain qualifications, of whom a bishop selected one. Now, they were anxious to have as master a gentleman with whom the bishop had a personal quarrel. They therefore looked about to find a co-nominee in the most utterly disreputable person who was duly qualified. They succeeded in finding one who had every fault that a man could have. His character was so thoroughly and undeniably disgraceful that no one, as they supposed, could for a moment even think of presenting him to any decent office. They nominated him with their favourite, hoping by this ingenious device to force their favourite upon the bishop. The bishop seeing that, if this were permitted, it would make his power of selection practically void, took them in their own trap. He appointed the disreputable nominee, who lived with a persistence as discreditable as his character, and for many years bore rule over the unhappy fellows.

To obtain an office simply by force of bad character is, however, a curious felicity given to few, and the paths which lead to the eminence are generally of a more agreeable character. The appointment is in almost every case in the hands of the fellows. In one case it belongs to the Crown, and the result is, as I must add, that the office has there been conferred upon the greatest living ornament to the University. Everywhere else, some dozen or twenty gentlemen meet to elect to one of the most desirable offices in England. If they were appointing a fellow or a scholar, they would choose him, as I have before explained, with the most scrupulous fairness. They would attend to no earthly consideration except his distinction in the appointed examinations.

But in election of a master they have no sense of responsibility whatever; they think no more of his fitness for the place than a Lord Chancellor thinks of the fitness of a candidate for a clerkship in the House of Lords, or a patron of the fitness of his son for a living; and, indeed, it would be difficult to define the qualities which fit a man for an office where the chief duty of a man consists in consulting his own comfort in a dignified manner. It is looked upon, in fact, as a pure piece of plunder, and various more or less authentic anecdotes are current of the means by which it is attained. The most creditable and the most common motive in such a small society is, of course, private friendship. But even in our immaculate societies, private interest is not quite insensible. Twelve fellows, for example, meet in a room. On examining the votes it appears that every candidate has received one vote, whilst none receives two, and the candidates are identical with the electors. After several scrutinies, leading to the same unsatisfactory result, A. takes B. aside, and points out that if A. becomes master, B.'s many merits will infallibly recommend him for the office of tutor (the appointment to which is in the hands of the master). At the next scrutiny each of the

other candidates still receives one vote, A. has two
and B. none, and A. accordingly is elected master.

How much truth may be shadowed forth in this
or in some more modern scandals, I am unable
to say. The most powerful recommendation of a
candidate is, however, as a rule, the possession or
the prospect of the best college living. In the first
case, a vacancy is made in a place which above all
others is apt to produce in expectant candidates
the sickness of hope deferred. The strongest point
made in the late controversy as to whether any one
had ever been known to have reached the age of
a hundred, was the fact that no college incumbent
was known to have done so. The indomitable per-
severance with which these gentlemen continue to
live, without the least regard to the feelings of
their would-be successors, is one of the most
lamentable and best established facts of human
nature. If you cannot remove one of them to a
higher sphere, the next best thing is to elect some
one who stands in your way. It follows that in
this, as in some other walks of life, the best means
of gaining one office is to be in possession or imme-

diate expectation of another. As one vote may easily
turn the scale when there are so few voters, this is
very often the deciding cause.

For a small body of men, most of them intimately
known to each other, to select one of their number
to a post which imposes next to no duties and confers
considerable advantages, is obviously an invidious
task. The cardinals are said to have an unpleasant
time of it in electing the Pope ; and I doubt whether
they are filling up a more desirable office. The Pope,
we all know, leads a happy life ; he drinks the best
of Rhenish wine, and only suffers from the evils of
enforced celibacy. The more fortunate head of a
house acquires on his election not merely additional
facilities for the cultivation of a good cellar of wine,
but he has the privilege, and almost the duty of
taking a wife. As the only married man among
a corporation of bachelors, he ought to feel even
more keenly than other men the advantages of
matrimony. He settles down in his little kingdom,
and devotes himself to such studies and amusements
as befit the dignity of his exalted position. His
fellows may laugh at him, or make epigrams upon

him in secret. Young men are apt to be irreverent. But their idle murmurs can hardly penetrate from the combination room to the lodge of the august object of ridicule. He is probably popular as the superior officers in a regiment or the head officials in a department are popular, although their subalterns or clerks think it the correct thing to rail at them. Indeed, he is generally looked upon with respect, sometimes with admiration, and always with envy.

Meanwhile he dispenses such elegant hospitality, according to the established phrase, as he chooses at those sublime entertainments where wretched undergraduates stand trembling in their shoes and deep professors discourse on lively scientific topics. He does as much University business as he likes, which sometimes means a great deal, and sometimes means that he sits solemnly upon certain boards which meet once a term to settle that no change need be made in the University system ; and he devotes the remainder of his time to studies of so abstruse a character, or into which he plunges so profoundly, that he seldom manages to bring them to a close within the term of his natural life.

I think I have said enough to prove that an office which combines so much ease with so much dignity is an ornament to the University, and to call down indignation upon some rash reformers who once ventured to propose the " exploitation," or, as they coarsely expressed it, the utilization of master-ships—a term only fit to apply to sewage. Radicals of this destructive character would soon proclaim themselves unable to see the merits of a constitutional monarch. They would insist upon his governing as well as reigning.

To conclude the subject of our great authorities, I must add a few words upon professors. An immense deal of talk has been expended upon our professoriate, which in other places constitutes the whole teaching body of the University, but which at Cambridge has been pushed out of place and reduced to a small compass by the tutorial system. I am not going to argue or even to hint at any arguments about University reform. I will only remark that the insignificance of the part played by professors follows from a very simple principle, which I have endeavoured to explain elsewhere.

Our plan is not to teach any one anything, but to offer heavy prizes for competition in certain well-defined intellectual contests. As most of the professors lecture upon topics which have no particular bearing upon those contests, upon Sanskrit perhaps, or Archæology, or History, or Political Economy, or some equally useless and absurd subject, few people go to hear them. They would not be a bit more likely to win the prizes we offer if they did; and we have, as I have remarked, a healthy contempt for any knowledge which does not directly pay.

We are, therefore, obliged to legislate to provide the professors with hearers; as we don't wish to interfere with the studies of our best men, we fill their rooms with the worst. Young gentlemen, for example, who are studying theology, which generally means young gentlemen who are not studying at all, have to attend some twenty lectures. I earned eternal gratitude from the Divinity Professor, whom I honoured with my attendance, by a simple device. I wished to learn shorthand; and, consequently, whilst some ninety-nine of his class were engaged in sleeping,

or making surreptitious bets, or sketching flattering
portraits of the lecturer, I was always to be seen
taking voluminous notes with desperate eagerness.
I confess that I have never referred to them since;
but that professor, though now a dean, always stops
to speak to me, and I can see that my delicate
flattery still touches his memory.

Other professors are provided with a still
inferior material. Poll men are compelled to
attend a course of lectures, and to pass an examination in them afterwards. To pluck a man
once for ignorance in these examinations is considered cruel; but to pluck him twice is an almost
unheard-of severity. It follows that the standard of
attention is not very high. An energetic professor
of course enforces order upon his roomful of
ignorant and idle youths, who come to him precisely
because they are ignorant and idle. Even this is not
always the case. A professor who took the names
of the attending class at the end of his lecture found
that a large proportion came in fifty-five minutes
after the beginning. He then took the names at the
beginning, and found that before the end, half had

oozed out through the door. He locked the door, and a new route of escape was discovered through the window. The window was secured, and the consequence was probably a greater increase of attendance than of attention. Some gentlemen, however, possess the art of attracting hearers without compulsion, and as a rule, our young men submit to the infliction, sufficiently senseless, with remarkable good grace.

I will only add that our professors are ill paid, because the University, as distinguished from the colleges, is very poor; that they are a body of men of whom on other grounds we have a right to be proud, and that they give, in addition to these courses, other excellent lectures, of which the only complaint to be made is that they are too often delivered to very bare benches. I hope that things will soon be placed on a more satisfactory footing.

XII.

CONCLUSION.

I MIGHT add many other sketches to my limited gallery. I have not attempted to exhaust my materials, but to select a few of our most characteristic types. Many species must, so far as I am concerned, go without a natural historian. With some I am but slightly acquainted, and some are so poor in individuals that I could not describe them without personality.

Thus I am conscious of one obvious deficiency. Oxford and Cambridge are, in the eyes of Dissenters, hotbeds of unhealthy forms of belief; they shoot out feelers towards Rome, and are not unaffected by the blight of Germanism, neologism, and various other isms of vague but diabolical intentions. Good old Churchmen, on the other hand, consider us to be the great stronghold of religion qualified by decent education; "scholars and gentlemen" are still turned out from our manufactories as some counterpoise to the prevailing glut of "literates." We furnish arms to the youthful warriors who go out to smite the Zulu hip and thigh, and teach them to despise the gewgaws of a bastard Romanism spread to entice them from the path of duty. I could almost rise to eloquence on the subject after a perusal of certain religious journals. We must be, without knowing it, the common recruiting district of hostile sects. Jesuits in disguise are mining underground; silly Tractarians are touting for mock monasteries; wily infidels are spreading insidious unbelief.

Surely, where such hostile and excited rivals meet to snap their prey, as it were, out of each other's jaws, strong feelings must be generated; some remarkable character must be brought out in the contest; and I might even gain the thanks of the *Record*—or, better still, its abuse—by unmasking some of the leaders of proselytism.

I have heard one or two stories which lead me to suppose that there are actually a few persons answering to the descriptions of the volunteer detectives of Protestant journals. There is, or was, a society calling itself a Church Union (I think), which used, or used not, to commit some kind of periodical absurdity in the way of consecrating gyp-rooms, and walking in processions. A journal, universally known for its wisdom as " Solomon," occasionally denounced them eloquently, and for aught I know, justly.

There may, again, possibly be a few rash men who don't "receive for gospel what the Church believes," though, if so, they do not obtrude their incredulity upon us. If our evangelicals are not so manly as in the days of Simeon and the Clapham sect, if their oratory has become rather small beer or is a trifle sour, still they are supposed to exist. I occasionally get an invitation to prayer meetings conducted by undergraduates, and hear of rather fiery denunciations of worldly-minded persons—that is, of persons who can't be brought to believe in certain dismal prospects of all except true Protestants. But our prevailing tone is what I should venture to describe as one of quiet good sense, and what fanatics would consider to be only fit for careless. Gallios.

We differ strangely from Oxford in this respect, if I may judge from the reports of newspapers. Our brethren there seem to be always indulging in battles royal; the clergy hastening to rally round the Church in danger, and Liberals to support freedom of opinion. They keep up organized parties. They swear by Dr. Pusey, or fight under the banners of Dr. Stanley. They have theological controversies, and care which gets the best of them. They argue desperately and long whether a gentleman is orthodox enough to be allowed five hundred a year for teaching Greek.

It is not so with us. I might argue that the explanation lies in a statement which I found lately in Mr. Lecky's excellent work on Rationalism. Oxford, he says, has always violently opposed every theological movement, which has proved to be ultimately successful. I might attribute all their exciting contests to the fury of a few bigots, rushing like bulls at a gate at all progressive action. The Liberals, I might say, are rendered energetic by the necessity of holding their own against the reactionary torrent. I do not, however, accept this as a fact, nor, if it were a fact, would the cause of this unfortunate propensity be much more evident. I am content to assume, what is, I think, an indisputable truth at present, whatever its origin, that political and theological contests excite an interest at Oxford which is quite unknown to us. This distinction is connected with a difference of tone between the two Universities, which strikes the philosophical observer.

The model Oxford reformer is of a breed comparatively rare amongst us. If I may say it without offence, we are of a coarser and rougher texture. He is apt to be a democrat in kid gloves; he propounds revolutionary sentiments, sufficient to make a bishop's hair bristle on his head, in a subdued and lady-like voice. He admires metaphysics and general principles, and is apt to be, in our opinion, rather too hairsplitting and refined for practice. His fault is that, if anything, he inclines to the coxcombry of politics. We despise, or, at any rate, care little for abstract disquisition. Representing in this respect the commoner English type, we have the strongest objection to look far beyond our noses. We take what lies next to us and don't trouble our heads about its remoter bearings. Our studies are all modelled in accordance with a strictly practical view of the matter, that is, as I have said before, with a view to affording a good test for examinations; and we are inclined to sneer at loftier but more aërial considerations. Our ideal takes in the good and the bad points of rough, vigorous, common sense; whereas the Oxford man is not content without a touch of more or less refined philosophy. We generally take a narrower, but what is commonly called a more practical view of matters.

Which of these two types is the best is not for me to say; but the distinction which I have endeavoured to describe runs through all our manifestations to a marked degree. Mr. Gladstone, with his great abilities somewhat marred by over-acuteness and polish, is an excellent type of the Oxford mind. We have unluckily no such political representative; but perhaps I might mention Lord Macaulay, with his clear and energetic, but limited intellect, as, in many respects, a fair specimen of the Cambridge tone of thought.

One consequence of this is our greater fertility in what I have called the careless Gallios. The movement led by Doctor Newman scarcely stirred our sober minds. *Essays and Reviews* have not seriously troubled our repose. We leave theology to theologians, and mind our classics and mathematics. We introduce reforms when we want them and make no fuss about them. Part of our immunity indeed from party discussions has been owing to the fact that we have had much fewer reforms to make in the colleges or in the University than were found necessary at Oxford. We had no foundations to throw open, and were quite content with our educational system.

Whether this comparative calmness is taken for a sign of stagnation or of a healthy condition, I shall not inquire further. But it is conducive to pleasant society. A Gallio is generally a pleasant companion. Many are the pleasant evenings which have been partially spoilt for me during the last four years by discussions about the American war. It was the one topic upon which no human being could keep his temper. When the word secession was mentioned, faces began to grow red and voices loud, and I braced myself up for a vigorous talking match. If for no other reason, I should have delighted to hear of General Lee's surrender, as opening a prospect of peace in our combination rooms as well as across the Atlantic ; for it now turns out that every one sympathized more or less with the North, and decidedly prophesied their success from the very beginning.

But at Cambridge, even when the discussions were at their wildest, when my best friends would hardly speak to me after a Northern victory, and when I slunk out of the way after a Northern defeat, there was always a means of escape. It was only necessary to turn the conversation upon theology to smooth the troubled waters.

This would, I believe, be a dangerous expedient in a country parish, or possibly in some other places. But at Cambridge I have always found that it is a topic which every one can discuss in perfect good temper except the few whom it sends to sleep.

I may, then, obtain credit for the boast that
Cambridge is a pleasant place to inhabit for those
who do not object to bachelor society. The one
thing that can spoil the social intercourse of well-
educated men, living in great freedom from unnecessary etiquette, is a spirit of misplaced zeal. We
have, as, indeed, every society has, a certain amount
of " shop " to be talked. Approaching examinations,
A.'s prospect of succeeding to a college living, and
B.'s of becoming a bishop, have to be discussed, as
lawyers talk of briefs and doctors of interesting cases.
But we are distracted by no violent parties; no one
has ever tried to convert me, nor, so far as I know,
considered me an outcast and a reprobate for refusing
to be converted. We have therefore every reason for
making a good use of our large opportunities for
social meeting. In London you are separated from
your most intimate friend by half an hour's drive,
and meet him late in the evening for two or three
hours on your good behaviour. In Cambridge, besides the power of dropping in at any time in the
morning for the trouble of crossing a court, you are
expected often to dine at five and pass the rest of the

evening in conversation not uncheered by the cigar or even the " churchwarden" of domestic life.

As the units of our society are separated by few party distinctions, and are constantly meeting on the most friendly terms, they form an agreeable whole, with but one drawback. That, I need not say, is the absence of ladies' society; but I shall not venture to say how far or in what respects I consider it to be a drawback at all. For already the action of the commissioners has begun to be felt; ladies are no longer those rarely seen beings who come to wonder at and to enliven us at intervals in the May term. Married fellows and married tutors are becoming common. It is hardly safe to find any fault with the change. But perhaps I may hint in the most delicate manner that a little regret may be felt at this incipient breaking-up of a very pleasant though peculiar form of society. I never held that, in the words of the candidate for orders, matrimony was a fond thing, vainly invented, and resting upon no certain warranty of Scripture; but it certainly rather tends to destroy the strong college spirit which formed such a pleasant bond of union; a married fellow will, I fear, oftener think more of his wife than his college, and the high table at which we now meet daily will be the worse for the loss of communistic spirit. Possibly, we may not be quite so much at ease with each other; the respectable gentlemen who don't mind meeting me and hearing my opinions may think them not fitted for their wives.

But I will not speculate further on such a dangerous topic. I will conclude what I have to say on this and on the University generally, by confessing that I have enjoyed so many pleasant hours in it under its present constitution, that I feel a conservative shrinking from any proposals of change.

THE END.

Printed in the United States
By Bookmasters